THE HINDU REALISM

THE HINDU REALISM

BEING AN INTRODUCTION TO THE METAPHYSICS OF THE NYAYA-VAISHESHIKA SYSTEM OF PHILOSOPHY

BY

JAGADISHA CHANDRA CHATTERJI

GYAN

Published by

GYAN

Gyan Publishing House
5, Ansari Road
Daryaganj, New Delhi-110002
Phone: 011-47034999, 9811692060
E-mail: books@gyanbooks.com

Distribution Network
gyanbooks.com
India, USA, Canada, UK, Australia

ISBN: 978-93-6433-391-7 (HB)
First Published, 1908

2nd Impression 2024

Printed at: Gyan Press, Delhi.

THE HINDU REALISM
Author: JAGADISHA CHANDRA CHATTERJI

HINDU REALISM

HINDU REALISM

BEING

AN INTRODUCTION TO THE METAPHYSICS OF THE NYÂYA-VAISHEṢHIKA SYSTEM OF PHILOSOPHY

BY

JAGADÎSHA CHANDRA CHATTERJI, B.A. (CANTAB.),

VIDYÂVÂRIDHI,

DIRECTOR OF THE ARCHÆOLOGICAL AND RESEARCH DEPARTMENT
KASHMIR STATE.

ALLAHABAD

THE INDIAN PRESS

1912

CONTENTS.

PREFACE.

In the following pages* I have made an attempt to present the main *metaphysical* doctrines of two of the Hindu Schools of Philosophy, the Vaisheṣhika and the Nyâya, constituting what may be called Hindu Realism.

The attempt has been made after I have tried, during my residence at Cambridge, to understand and assimilate the European attitude in matters philosophical and the European mode of philosophic thinking.

I have not made any explicit comparison between the Realism, or any other phase, of European thinking and the Realism of the Hindus; but I have always kept the European ideas and attitude before my mind, so as to make this presentation of Hindu Realism intelligible to the Western reader.

Although written as early as 1824, and with insufficient material before him, yet the Essay of Colebrooke† on the Nyâya-Vaisheṣhika is still perhaps the best work on the subject in any European language. But excellent as the essay is, Colebrooke wrote it as a philologist more than a philosopher; and I doubt very much if a

---

* Being my thesis written as an 'Advanced Student' of the Cambridge University. Its publication has been greatly delayed as I have been wanting to add to it at least two more parts, namely, on the Sâṅkhya and the Vedânta. But pressure of other duties has as yet left me no time to accomplish this although, in so far as the Sâṅkhya is concerned, I have done it partially in my *Kashmir Shaivaism* which is now in the press and will be very shortly published in the *Kashmir Series of Texts and Studies* edited by myself.

† Republished in 1873 in 'Essays,' Vol. II.

Western student of philosophy can at all get from it an intelligent idea of the Hindu system.

And if the earliest essay on the subject is not, nor was perhaps intended to be, a *rational* presentation of the Nyâya-Vaisheṣhika system, neither is the latest a reasoned statement of the case. For I am equally doubtful if, by reading Professor Max Müller's account of the system, a European student of philosophy can form an idea as to the *reason* or *reasons* why the Hindu Realists held, and do hold even now, the *metaphysical* doctrines which are taught in their system.*

As for the translations of original Sanskrit works on the system, they can hardly be understood by anyone but those Orientalists themselves who are, or must be, already well acquainted with the Hindu mode of thinking and Hindu terminology.†

In regard to these translations Dr. Thibaut says:—

"Indian Philosophy would, in my opinion, be more readily and widely appreciated than it is at present, if the translators of philosophical works had been somewhat more concerned to throw their versions into a form less strange and repellent to the Western reader than literal renderings from technical Sanskrit must needs be."—(Thibaut's translation of the Shrî Bhâṣhya, p. x.)

Thus it happens that there is hardly a single presentation, in a European language, of the *metaphysics* of the

---

* Max Müller's Six Systems of Indian Philosophy, 1899. Reprinted 1903.

† Translations—Nyâya Sûtras, Books I-IV., by Ballantyne, with extracts from the Vṛitti; Vaisheṣhika Sûtras in English by Gough, in German by Roer; Tarka Sangraha by Ballantyne, Bhâṣhâ-Parich. by Roer.

Nyâya-Vaisheṣhika which would enable the reader to understand properly the *reasoning* by which it is supported. This honour I venture to claim for the present attempt, which is made by me not as a philologist, or an orientalist, but as a student of philosophy.

(*a*) The first claim then in regard to the originality of the following pages is that they contain a *rational* presentation, for the first time in a European language, of Hindu Realism *generally*.

(*b*) And in regard to special points, I venture to think that the following are presented for the first time in an intelligible form to a Western reader :—

(i) The idea of the Paramâṇus—an idea which is considered to be the most characteristic of the Nyâya-Vaisheṣhika.

(ii) The idea of Kâla.

(iii) The idea of Dik.

(*c*) In addition to these claims to originality, this presentation of Hindu Realism also includes :—

(i) A fuller (though not exhaustive) statement, than is to be found in any other work in a European language, of the arguments given in support of the Âtman from the Nyâya-Vaisheṣhika point of view.

(ii) A fuller and more intelligent presentation of the "Synthetic Aspect" from the Realistic standpoint.

I have confined myself to the explanation of the main doctrines only as taught by Kaṇâda and Gotama, and have left out several of the minor ones, such as that of 'Samavâya,' which is peculiar to the Vaisheṣhika and the key to its notion of causality, *i.e.*, the relation between the producing source and the product. I have also left out entirely all the later ideas; but I have given some of the recent *reasonings* which have been advanced on the subject by living and genuinely Hindu thinkers to meet objections based on European thought.

In presenting Hindu Realism, I have placed myself in the position of a Realist and a genuine follower of Kaṇâda and Gotama. To write and speak as though one fully believed in the doctrines one has to present has been an ancient Hindu attitude. It was in this attitude that the great Vâchaspati Mishra wrote on almost all the schools of Hindu Philosophy.

I subjoin herewith a list of the authorities, mostly in original Sanskrit, which I have consulted and referred to in support of my interpretation of the system.

I have left out all consideration of the 'history' of the system, or of its literature. European scholars have written on the subject; but as they have written with their own notion of the "philosophy of history" and with pre-conceptions which are peculiar to the Western mind, the history as conceived by them can be, from the Hindu standpoint, but partial truth (*see* pp. 130, 131 and 155). Still it serves all practical purposes and I have therefore refrained from touching upon the subject. But the list of the authorities subjoined is so arranged as to give one some idea of the history of the system in so far as its present literature is concerned.*

* For a history, from the Western standpoint, of the system, *see* also Introduction to Tharka-Saṅgraha, by M. R. Boḍas, in the Bombay Sanskrit Series.

In this connection it may be just noted that the age of the existing *works* is no guide to the age and origin of the *system* itself (see note 5). The Hindus regard the whole of their Smṛiti literature, to which the Darshana-Shâstra (their philosophy) belongs, as a branch of learning in which the meaning only is of importance (artha-pradhâna) and distinguish it sharply from the Vedas or Shruti in which the words or sounds are of importance (shabda-pradhâna).* They can therefore see how it is possible that the Smṛiti literature, while retaining the meanings or ideas, has yet changed its form again and again, and how it is also possible that the Shruti, in so far as it is preserved, has retained its very words and sounds. In these circumstances, they hold that any system of their philosophy as a system of thoughts and ideas may be much older than the existing books in which it is now contained.

I have given most of the references in the foot-notes; but where a reference has needed some explanation I have given the same in notes at the end.

As the notes are often of the nature of textual criticisms or elucidation of texts, and can be needed to justify my statements to Sanskritists only, I have left many a word and passage untranslated.

Trinity College, Cambridge,
March 1908.

J. C. CHATTERJI.

* I got this idea from one of my teachers, M. M. Paṇḍit Chandrakânta Tarkâlaṅkâra.

LIST OF AUTHORITIES AND SOURCES.

THE VAISHEṢHIKA.

1. i. The Vaisheṣhika Sûtras of Kaṇâda. Pub., Ben. Sans. Ser. For editions used *see* below. The oldest existing work on the subject. The old commentaries on the Sûtras are lost, at least not found yet.

2. ii. Prashastapâda's Padârtha-Dharma-Saṅgraha ; for edition used *see* below.

3. iii. Udayanâchârya's Kiraṇâvalî, Comm. on the above. Only part of this work (as far as section on Dik) with corresponding texts of Prashastapâda has been published in the Ben. Sans. Ser. with extracts from Vardhamâna's Kiraṇâvalî-prakâsha. The rest of this work has been consulted in Mss.

4. iv. Shrîdhara's Nyâya-Kandalî, another Comm. on Prashastapâda, published with the latter in the Viz. Sans. Ser., Ben. An excellent edition.

5. v. Lakṣhaṇâvalî by Udayanâchârya—giving definitions of Vaisheṣhika terms. Published (the text only) as an appendix to No. 3. (Udayana and Shrîdhara were very likely contemporaries).

6. vi. Saptapadârthî by Shivâditya or Vyoma Shivâchârya. If by latter, it will

precede Udayana's works. It may be regarded also as a work on both Vaish. and Nyâya jointly. For edition used *see* below.

7. vii. Upaskâra, Comm. on the Vaisheṣhika Sûtras of Kaṇâda by Shaṅkara Mishra (pub. in Bib. Ind.).

8. viii. Vivṛiti by Jayanârâyaṇa, Com. on No. 1. Pub. together with Nos. 7 and 1 in Bib. Ind.

9. ix. A Comm. on No. 1, with what is said to be the Bhâradvâja Vṛitti (one of the old and now lost commentaries on the Sûtras), by Gaṅgâdhara Kaviratna-Kavirâja. It is impossible to distinguish in this work the Bhâradvâja Vṛitti (if there is any of it in the work) from what is actually written by Gaṅgâdhara himself. Its reading of the Sûtras and their arrangement are widely different from the other commentaries mentioned above. Pub. Berhampore (Murshidabad) Shak. 1790. The copy I have used is in the India Office Library (I. B. L. 13), London.

10. x. Chandrakântîya Bhâṣhya, Comm. on No. 1 by M. M. Chandrakânta Tarkâlaṅkâra, a living author;* formerly professor in the Government Sanskrit College, Calcutta (one of my teachers). Pub. Calcutta, 1887.

---

* Since dead.

THE NYÂYA.

11. i. Nyâya Sûtras of Gotama, oldest existing work on the subject. Published as an appendix to Fasc. No. 4, of the Nyâya-Vârttika in Bib. Ind., 1897. For other editions used *see* below.

12. ii. Nyâya-Bhâṣhya by Vâtsyâyana or Pakṣhilasvâmin. Earliest existing Comm. on No. 11. Published with the Sûtras and numerous extracts from Nos. 13 and 14, in the Viz. Sans. Ser. An excellent edition.

13. iii. Nyâya-Vârttika by Udyotakara, supplementary to, and elucidation of No. 12 ; written when Buddhism was greatly flourishing in India, *i.e.*, the early centuries of the Christian era. Published in 6 parts or fasces in the Bib. Ind., 1887-1904.

14. iv. Nyâya-Vârttika-Tâtparya-Ṭîkâ by Vâchaspati Mishra ; explanatory to Nos. 12 and 13. Pub. in Viz. Sans. Ser.

15. v. Nyâya-Mañjarî by Jayanta Bhaṭṭa ; pub. in Viz. Sans. Ser. This may be regarded almost as an encyclopædia of the Nyâya system.

16. vi. Nyâya-Vṛitti by Vishvanâtha ; a Comm. on No. 11. Pub. first in Calcutta, 1828. But the edition used by me is that published by Jîvânanda. It is from this that extracts were translated by Ballantyne.

17. vii. Târkika-Rakṣhâ, by Varadarâja. (For edition used *see* below.)

Of these works, Nos. 1-5 are of the greatest importance on the Vaisheṣhika. Nos. 6-8 are also of great weight and authority. No. 9 is not much known. No. 10 is the work of perhaps the greatest living Paṇḍit of Bengal. On the Nyâya, Nos. 11 to 14 are of the greatest authority. Nos. 15 and 16 too are of much weight.

NYÂYA-VAISHEṢHIKA.

18. i. Bhâṣha-Parichchheda by Vishvanâtha. Ed. Bib. Ind.

19. ii. Siddhânta-Muktâvalî, Comm. on the above by Vishvanâtha himself. Bib. Ind.

20. iii. Tarka-Saṅgraha by Annambhaṭṭa. Ed. Bom. Sans. Ser. by Y. V. Aṭhalye and M. R. Boḍas.

OTHER WORKS ON THE NYÂYA AND THE VAISHEṢHIKA.

21. i. Mitabhâṣhiṇî, Comm. on No. 6; published with No. 6 in Viz. Sans. Ser.

22. ii. Niṣhkaṇṭaka, Comm. on No. 17; pub. with same, first in the Pandit and then in book form by Lazarus & Co., Benares.

23. iii. Siddhânta-Chandrodaya, Comm. on No. 20, by Shrîkṛiṣhṇa Dhûrjaṭî, B enares, 1881. (Oblong edition.)

Works on the other systems.

THE SÂṄKHYA-YOGA.

24. i. The Sâṅkhya-Kârikâs.

25. ii. Gauḍapâda's Comm. on same.

26. iii. Vâchaspati Mishra's Sâṅkhya-Tattva-Kaumudî, Comm. on No. 24.

27. iv. Sâṅkhya-Chandrikâ, Comm. on No. 24 by Nârâyaṇa. Pub. at Benares.

28. v. The Sâṅkhya-Sûtras.
29. vi. The Sâṅkhya-Pravachana-Bhâṣhya by Vijñânabhikṣhu. Comm. on No. 28.
30. vii. Vṛitti by Aniruddha on No. 28. Garbe's edition.
31. viii. Yoga-Sûtras of Patañjali.
32. ix. Bhâṣhya on the above; Ed. by Râjarâma Shâstrî, Bombay.
33. x. Vyâkhyâ by Vâchaspati Mishra on No. 32. (All three pub. by Jîvânanda.)
34. xi. Yoga-Vârttika by Vijñânabhikṣhu; Comm. on No. 32, pub. in the Pandit by Lazarus.
34a. xii. Karma-Mîmâṁsâ with Bhâṣhya.

THE VEDÂNTA.

35. i. Brahma-Sûtras.
36. ii. Shârîraka-Bhâṣhya by Shaṅkarâchârya on the above.
37. iii. Ratna-Prabhâ by Govindânanda on No. 36.
38. iv. Bhâmatî by Vâchaspati Mishra on No. 36.

(All these, together with another gloss by Ânanda Giri, pub. by the Nirṇaya Sâgara Press, Bombay, 1904; an excellent edition.)

39. v. Shrî-Bhâṣhya, Com. on No. 35. Pub. with Shruta-prakâshikâ by Lazarus & Co., Benares, in three vols.
40. vi. Vivaraṇopanyâsa by Râmânanda Sarasvatî. Ben. Sans. Ser.
41. vii. Advaita-Brahma-Siddhi by Sadânanda; Bib. Ind.

OTHER PHILOSOPHICAL WORKS.

42. i. Âtmatattva-viveka by Udayana, containing a refutation of the Buddhistic notions in regard to the Âtman. Edition used is by Jîvânanda, Calcutta, 1873.

43. ii. Shiva-Sûtra-Vimarṣhiṇî, an ancient work on the Shaiva philosophy as taught in Kashmir. Edited by myself.

44. iii. Hindu Philosophy in 5 vols., being S.G.V.M. Fellowship lectures (Calcutta University) by M. M. Chandrakânta Tarkâlaṅkâra, in highly Sanskritised Bengali. Being the work of the most learned Paṇḍit of Bengal, it is at once of great authority and full of information.

45. iv. Sâṅkhya-Tattvâloka in Sanskrit and Bengali, by Svâmin Hariharânanda—one of the very few living Sâṅkhya-Sannyâsins of great learning and practical knowledge of Yoga.

46. v. Travels of Shivadhyâna. It is ıeally a philosophical work on the Sâṅkhya, written under the guise of the experiences of a Sannyâsin who travelled all over India and sojourned in the Himâlayas. It is one of the most remarkable works on the subject ever written. It is in Bengali. The author does not disclose his name but one knows that it is by the writer of No. 45.

47. vi. A Rational Refutation of the Hindu Philosophical Systems by Nîlakaṇṭha Shâstrî Goreh, and trans. by F. Hall.

48. vii. Dialogues on the Hindu Philosophy by K. M. Banerjea.
49. viii. Colebrooke's Essays.
50. ix. Six Systems of Indian Philosophy by Prof. F. Max Müller.
51. x. Die Sâṁkhya-Philosophie, by Prof. R. Garbe.

UPANIṢHADS, &c.

52. i. Muṇḍakopaniṣhat.
53. ii. Bṛihadâraṇyakopaniṣhat, with Com. by Shaṅkarâchârya.
54. iii. Bhagavad-Gîtâ.

PURÂṆAS, &c.

55. i. Mahâbhârata with Nîlakaṇṭha's Comm. (Calcutta edition, Pub. by the 'Baṅgabâsî' Press).
56. ii. Viṣhṇu Purâṇa.
57. iii. Bhâgavata.
58. iv. Manusaṁhitâ with Râghavânanda's Commentary on it.

BUDDHISTIC.

59. i. Dîgha-Nikâya.
60. ii. Majjhima-Nikâya (both Pub. by the Pâli Text Soc.).

GENERAL.

61. i. Shabda-Kalpa-Druma (A Sanskrit Dictionary).
62. ii. Medinî Koṣha.
63. iii. Prasthâna-Bheda by Madhusûdana Ṡarasvatî. Ed. and Pub. by Weber in his Indische Studien, Vol. I (1850).

64. iv. Niruktâlochana by Satyavrata Sâmashramin. Pub. in his edition of the Nirukta in Bib. Ind.

65. v. Chatruvarga-Chintâmaṇi, Bib. Ind.

TRANSLATIONS.

66. i. Vaish.-Sûtras with extracts from Comm., by Gough. (Lazarus & Co., Benares).

67. ii. *Ibid*, by Roer. (German) in Z.D. M. G., Vols. xxi, pp. 309-420; xxii, pp. 383-422; Leipzig, 1867, 1868.

68. iii. The Nyâya-Sûtras with extracts from the Vṛitti of Vishvanâtha by Ballantyne. Books I-IV only.

69. iv. The Vedânta-Sûtras by Dr. Thibaut in the Sacred Books of the East Series. Vols. xxxiv and xxxviii, containing the translation of the Shârîraka Bhâṣhya and Vol. xlviii, that of the Shrîbhâṣhya.

70. v. Bhâṣhâ-Parichchheda by Roer in Bib. Ind.

71. vi. The Yoga-Sûtras of Patañjali with Bhoja-Vṛitti by Râjâ Râjendralâla Mitra. Bib. Ind.

WESTERN WORKS.

72. i. Philosophy of History by Fred. von Schlegel. Eng. Trans. by J. B. Robertson, 1835.

73. ii. Appearance and Reality by Bradley.

74. iii. Some Dogmas of Religion by Dr. J. E. McTaggart.

75. iv. Multiple Personality by Drs. Sidis and Goodhart.

76. v. Evolution of Ethics by Huxley. Eversley Series, 1895.

ABBREVIATIONS USED.

Arranged alphabetically.

The number on the right is that of the work in the preceding 'List of Authorities and Sources,' p. ix.

Ad. Br. Sid.	=Advaita-Brahma-Siddhi ...	41
Ani.	=Aniruddha Vṛitti on the Sâṅkhya Sûtras...	30
Ât. Tat. Viv. ...	=Âtma-Tattva-Viveka ...	42
Banerjea Dial. H. Phil.	=Dialogues on the Hiṇḍu Philosophy	48
Ben. Sans. Ser.	=Benares Sanskrit Series.	
Bhâg.	=Bhâgavata	57
Bhag. Gîtâ. ...	=Bhagavad-Gîtâ	54
Bhâmatî ...	=Bhâmatî on Shâr. Bhâṣh. ...	38
Bhâṣhâ-Par. ...	=Bhâṣhâ-Parichchheda ...	18
Bib. Ind. ...	=Bibliotheca Indica.	
Bom. Sans. Ser.	=Bombay Sanskrit Series.	
Bradley App. & R.	=Appearance and Reality by Bradley	73
Brah. Sû. ...	=Brahma Sûtras	35
Bṛih. Up. ...	=Bṛihadâraṇyakopaniṣhat ...	53
Cha. Kâ. ...	=Hindu Philosophy by M. M. Chandra-Kânta	44
Chan. Bhâṣh. ...	=Chandrakântîya Bhâṣhya ...	10
Chatur Va. Chi. Ma.	=Chaturvarga Chintâmaṇi.	
Dîgh. Nik. ...	=Dîgha Nikâya	59
Dog. Rel. ...	=Some Dogmas of Religion ...	74
Gaṅgâ. ...	=Gaṅgâdhara's Commmentary ...	9
Gauḍ. Sâṅkh....	=Gauḍapâda's Commentary on Sâṅkhya Kârikâ	25
Goreh ...	=Rational Refutation by N. Shâstrî Goreh	47
Kandalî ...	=Nyâya-Kandalî	4
Ki. Va. ...	=Kiraṇâvalî	3

Ki. Va. Pr. ...	=Kiraṇâvalî-Prakâsha ...	3
Lakṣh. ...	=Lakṣhaṇâvalî	5
Ma. Bhâr. ...	=Mahâbhârata	55
Majj. Nik. ...	=Majjhima-Nikâya	60
Manu. ...	=Manu-Saṁhitâ	58
Medinî. ...	=Medinî Koṣha.	
Mit. ...	=Mitabhâṣhiṇî	21
Muṇḍ. Up. ...	=Muṇḍakopaniṣhat	52
N. V. T. Ṭ. ...	=Nyâya-Vârttika-Tâtparya-Ṭîkâ	14
Nyâ. Bhaṣh. ...	=Nyâya-Bhâṣhya	12
Nyâ. Mañj. ...	=Nyâya-Mañjarî	15
Nyâ. Sû. ...	=Nyâya-Sûtras	11
Nyâ. Vâr. ...	=Nyâya-Vârttika	13
Nyâ. Vṛit. ...	=Nyâya-Vṛitti	16
Pra. Bhe. ...	=Prasthâna-Bheda	63
Prashasta ...	=Prashastapâda's Padârtha-Dharma-Saṅgraha	2
Râjarâma ...	=Yoga-Sûtra, edited by Paṇḍit Râjarâma Shâstrin ...	32
Ration. Refut.	=Rational Refutation ...	47
Rat. Pr. ...	=Ratna-Prabhâ	37
Roer ...	=Roer's translation of Bhâṣhâ-Parichchheda	70
Sâṅ. K. ...	=Sâṅkhya-Kârikâs	24
Sâṁkh. Phil. ...	=Sâṁkhya-Philosophie ...	51
Sâṅkh. T. L. ...	=Sâṇkhya-Tattvâloka ...	45
Sâṅ. Sû. ...	=Sâṅkhya-Sûtras	28
Saptap. ...	=Sapta-padârthî	6
Saptap. Mit. ...	=Mitabhâṣhiṇî	21
Sa. Sâ. Ni. ...	=Nîruktâlochana by Satyavrata Sâmashramin	64
Schlegel. Phil. Hist.	=Schlegel's Philosophy of History	72
Sha. Ka. ...	=Shabda-Kalpa-Druma ...	61
Shâr. Bhâṣh. ...	=Shârîraka Bhâṣhya... ...	36
Shi. Dh. ...	=Travels of Shiva-Dhyâna ...	46

Shiv. S. Vim. ...	=Shiva-Sûtra-Vimarṣhiṇî ..	43
Shrî. Bhâṣh. ...	=Shrî-Bhâṣhya	39
Sid. Cha. ...	=Siddhânta-Chandrodaya ...	23
Sid. M. V. ...	=(Nyâya)-Siddhânta-Muktâvalî ...	19
Tark. Saṅ. ...	=Tarka-Saṅgraha	20
Târ. Rak. ...	=Târkika-Rakṣhâ	17
Thibaut ...	=Thibaut's translation of the Vedânta Sûtras, Shârîraka Bhâṣhya and Shrî-Bhâṣhya ...	69
Upask. ...	=Upaskâra	7
Vaish. Sû. ...	=Vaisheṣhika-Sûtras	1
Ved. Ḍiṇ. ...	=Vedânta-Ḍiṇḍima.	
Vijñâna ...	=Sâṅkhya-Prav. Bhâṣhya ...	29
Viṣh. Pur. ...	= Viṣhṇu Purâṇa	56
Vivaraṇopa. ...	=Vivaraṇopanyâsa	40
Vivṛ. ...	=Vivṛiti	8
Viz. Sans. Ser.	=Vizianagram Sanskrit Series.	
Yoga Sû. ...	=Yoga-Sûtras.	31

KEY TO THE PRONUNCIATION

OF

SANSKRIT WORDS.

The order is that of the Sanskrit alphabet.

Vowels (only those needed for our present purpose).

a as in ced*a*r.

â as in f*a*ther.

i as in p*i*n.

î as in mar*i*ne.

u as in p*u*sh.

û as in r*u*de.

ṛi as in mer*ri*ly.

e as in th*e*re.

ai as in *ai*sle.

o as in s*o*.

au as in H*au*s (German) or *ou* in h*ou*se.

Consonants (only those needed here and which have peculiarities of sound.)

g always hard as in give.

gh as in sta*g-h*orn pronounced quickly.

ṅ as *ng* in sing.

ch always soft as in church.

chh as in chur*ch-h*all pronounced quickly.

ñ as *n* in bunch.

ṭ pronounced with tongue turned up (cerebral.)

ṭh as in an*t-h*ill pronounced quickly.

ḍ pronounced with tongue turned up (cerebral).

ṇ cerebral.

t as in French.

th like th in *th*ank without any hissing sound.

d as in French.

dh the above aspirated.

ph as in philosophy.

bh as in sta*b*-*h*im pronounced quickly.

sh as s in sure.

ṣh pronounced like the above but with the tip of the tongue turned upward (cerebral).

ṁ nasal, not unlike ng in song.

ḥ aspirate.

HINDU REALISM

INTRODUCTORY.

(a)—General.

The name Hindu seems only to be a corrupt form of the Sanskrit Sindhu, *i.e.*, the Indus. It was in all probability given by the ancient Persians to those contemporaries of theirs who inhabited the provinces of India bordering on that river. Whatever the origin of the name, and however much one may dislike it personally owing to its history and associations, I must use it here; and by Hindus I shall mean all those people or peoples who accept, or did accept, that social polity and religious discipline which in Sanskrit is known as the Varṇâshrama Dharma and is based on the teachings of what is called the Veda—both these terms being explained later.*

The name Hindu defined.

By *Hindu Philosophy* I mean that branch of the ancient learning of the Hindus (in the above sense) which *demonstrates* by reasoning *propositions* in regard to (*a*) *what a man ought to do*, in order to gain true happiness

Hindu Philosophy defined.

* *Infra*, p. 131 and p. 132.

in and under particular circumstances and in specific states of existence; or (*b*) *what he ought to realise by direct experience*, in order to be radically and absolutely freed from suffering and to be absolutely independent —such propositions *being already given*, and lines of reasoning in their support being established, by duly qualified authorities, as also explained later on.*

Sanskrit names for philosophy.

In Sanskrit, Philosophy has been variously named; but it is at present chiefly known as Darshana Shâstra, which literally means the *science of views*, *i.e.*, correct views, in regard to either of the two kinds of propositions named above; namely, those embodying what a man should do to be truly happy in and under particular circumstances and in specific states, *i.e.*, his duties (Karma or Dharma); or those enunciating the truths of the essential nature of things (Tattva), so that a man by realising them may be absolutely free and independent.

It is also called Vichâra-Shâstra or Manana-Shâstra, both these terms meaning the "Science of Rational Demonstration," namely, of *propositions* put forward in regard to either *duty* (Karma or Dharma) or *essential truths* (Tattva).†

It may be said to *correspond* to what in the West, that is, Europe and America, is generally understood by Philosophy, *in so far as the latter is only a rational demonstration* of what a man should do to truly better

* Sha. Ka., *Sub voce* 'Darshana'; Sa. Sâ. Ni., Vol. iv., ne. line 1; Goreh, p. 1, para. 1; *See* Note 1; *Infra*, p. 3.

† Sha. Ka., *Sub voce* 'Darshana'; Vivr., vi. ii. 16; Sa. Sâ. Ni., *Ibid.* Cha. Kâ., Vol. I., p. 102; *See* Note 2.

himself, or of ultimate verities which are already realised by experience as facts ; that is to say, in so far as Philosophy is *not mere speculation* in regard to such duties and verities. The full meaning of this qualification will be understood as we go on.

Two main divisions of Hindu Philosophy.

From the definition given above it is obvious that Hindu Philosophy falls into two broad divisions, namely :—

(1) Rational demonstration of propositions of duty, that is to say, what a man should or should not do in order to realise happiness, in some state of specific existence. (*See* pp. 131-133).

This is called the Dharma-mîmâṁsâ or Karma-mîmâṁsâ. We shall refer to it as Dharma-mîmâṁsâ.*

(2) Rational demonstration of propositions in regard to those truths about the fundamental nature of things which a man should realise by direct experience, to be absolutely freed from suffering and absolutely independent.

This division may be called Tattva-mîmâṁsâ. It is also termed Mokṣha-Darshana.† We shall call it simply Metaphysical Philosophy, and refer to the truths discussed therein as Metaphysical Truths.

While thus the two divisions are made in regard to their special subject-matter, yet the Dharma-mîmâṁsâ is not, and cannot be, entirely free from some reasoning about Metaphysical Truths. For the very propositions it has to discuss are based on these truths, one of which, the fundamental one, is discussed at some length in

* Cha. Kâ., Vol. I, p. 105 (implied).

† Shi. Dh., p. 1.

the main text-book of this branch of Hindu Philosophy. Several other Metaphysical Truths are taken for granted. Thus even Dharma-mîmâṁsâ has a metaphysical basis, and a particular metaphysical standpoint, the place of which we shall see presently.

Schools of Metaphysical Philosophy.

As for Metaphysical Philosophy, it is represented by a number of what are called Tantras or Nayas, words which may be translated as *schools*, using this term in a sense which is, as will be soon seen, somewhat different from that which it usually bears in connection with Philosophy in the West.*

There are several of these schools, but only five are regarded as fundamental. Their names are : —

(1) Vaisheṣhika,
(2) Nyâya,
(3) Sâṅkhya,
(4) Yoga,
and (5) Vedânta.

The others are regarded as, and may be easily shown to be, but variations of these five.

Three main systems.

As is well-known, the fundamental five schools again really represent, in so far as what may be called purely *theoretical truths* are concerned, three systems grouped as follows:

(1) Vaisheṣhika-Nyâya or Nyâya-Vaisheṣhika,
(2) Sâṅkhya-Yoga,
and (3) Vedânta.†

---

* Nyâ. Bhâṣh. I. 1. 4. N. V. T. Ṭ., p. 146, line 15 ; Ki. Va., p. 117, *Infra*, p. 7, *et seq.*

† Cha. Kâ., Vol. I, p. 113 ; Ad. Br, Sid., p. 2 ; Pra. Bhe,

As stated before, the Dharma-mîmâṁsâ has a metaphysical basis of its own, and so far as this basis is concerned, it is also reckoned as belonging to the first group, namely, the Nyâya-Vaisheṣhika.

Thus, in reality, there are only three metaphysical systems of the Hindus. These systems again are not considered as mutually contradictory. They are regarded as forming a graduated series in which the three systems form, as it were, three great *standards*, suited to different types or grades of minds,—different intellectual (and only intellectual) capacities and temperaments.

Hindu conception of philosophy; and certain preconceptions of the Hindus.

This position follows as an inevitable consequence of the very conception the Hindus have of Philosophy itself. What that conception is, has been already hinted at. It might perhaps be made a little clearer, by stating here certain ideas which are universally held by all Hindus. They may be considered the general preconceptions of the Hindu mind.* But they are preconceptions for which the Hindus have reasons, that are, to them, quite full and satisfactory. Without, however, giving any of these reasons here, I shall first just state what, to a Hindu, seem to be the corresponding preconceptions of the Western mind; and then just give the Hindu ones, so that the latter may be seen by opposition, as it were, in clear relief. The two sets of preconceptions are, as it will be seen, diametrically opposed to each other.

---

* *See* Note 3.

It seems to a Hindu that Western students of his Philosophy start generally with the following pre-suppositions, which are apparently assumed as established facts :—

(1) Man can never know Metaphysical Truths by *direct experience,* in the same way, for instance, as he can know sense objects. And, therefore, Metaphysical Truths can, at best, be but matters of *speculation* and mere *inferences* or only based on *faith.*

(2) Even if it be conceded, as a sort of possibility, that men may perhaps know these truths some day by direct experience, yet there has been so far no man who has known them in this fashion.

(3) Therefore, being matters of pure speculation, the various schools of Hindu philosophy, like any other speculative systems of the West, must be mutually contradictory, and if any one of them be true, the others must be false.

As against these, the Hindu preconceptions are :—*

(1) Man can *know* Metaphysical Truths, like any other truths, *by direct experience,* and not merely by speculation, by inference, or by faith.

(2) There *have been* men in the past who have thus known the whole truth of our nature and existence, as well as that of the Universe as a whole.

These men are known as Ṛiṣhis, which term, in this connection, may be translated as "perfected seers."†

(3) And, it is by knowing Metaphysical Truths by direct experience that some of the Ṛiṣhis have taught them to the Hindus.

---

* Cha. Kâ., Ad. Br. Sid., Goreh, &c. Note 3.

† See Note 4.

(4) But the Ṛishis have taught the Metaphysical Truths not as dogmas, to be received merely on faith, but by rational demonstration. That is to say, they have demonstrated *by reasoning** the truths, already realised by them as matters of direct and positive experience.

And it is this *rational* demonstration of, that is, demonstrating *by reasoning*, the metaphysical truths, which constitutes Philosophy according to the Hindu point of view.†

The function of Philosophy, therefore, is not the *discovery* of metaphysical truths, by reasoning and inference; but only the *explaining* and *understanding rationally* of such truths *already discovered* and *realised by experience.*‡

(5) These truths, being realised by the Ṛishis by direct experience, that is, *not* being conceived by them as matters of mere *speculation, inference,* or *faith,* all the Ṛishis have known them as the *same,* in much the same way as all who are provided with eyes may know the sun as one and the same thing.§

(6) But, while the metaphysical truths as realised by them are the same in every case, the Ṛishis have taught this one and the same set of truths, in what may be called three different *standards* or *grades,*|| which are represented by, but not necessarily exactly the same as, the great text-books known as the philosophical Sûtras.¶

---

* See Note 57. † *Ibid* ; also note 1.

‡ *Ibid.* and *infra*, p. 140. § Cha. Kâ., &c.

|| Pra Bhe., p. 23; Ad. Br. Sid., p. 151, lines 3 *et seq.* from bottom; Ât. Tat. Viv., pp. 131-132; Ved. Ḍiṇ., 19; Cha. Kâ., Vol. I, p. 6.; Râjarâma, Intro.; &c.

¶ *See* Note 5.

And they have thus taught *in order to* suit different minds, in much the same way as, say, the grammar of Sanskrit or Greek may be taught in different standards, such as practical, historical, philological, and so on.

(7) And it is these three different *standards of teaching and presenting rationally* one and the *same* body of essential truths, *already realised* by the Ṛiṣhis *by direct experience*, which constitute the three fundamental systems of Philosophy mentioned above.* They are therefore *not contradictory* to one another, but together form *a single and gradually advancing series*, in which, it may be pointed out, the order of the three systems *may* or *may not* be one of historical succession.

(8) Not only are not the three different standards of Philosophy contradictory to one another, but they all lead to the *same practical end.*† A man may pursue any one of them, according to his intellectual capacity and temperament, and yet reach the same practical end as others following the other standards. How this is possible may again be exemplified by our previous illustration of the different standards of the grammar of a language like Sanskrit. While what I have called the historical and philological standards of the grammar may give one a knowledge of the language respectively in its historical development and in regard to its ultimate sources, they, as well as the first standard, may give one a *practical* knowledge, *i.e.*, knowledge enabling one to speak and write the language correctly, which may be exactly the same. Similarly, while the second and third

---

* *Ante* p. 4.

† Ât. Tat. Viv., p. 1 ; Cha. Kâ, Vol. I, p. 6.

standards of Philosophy may, and indeed do, give one a good deal more of what may be called theoretical knowledge or knowledge of secondary importance, they, as well as the first standard, lead one to the same practical end which is the realisation of absolute freedom and independence.

That the Hindus regard their different systems as forming a gradually advancing series has not been entirely unknown in the West. It was known, in a more or less confused manner, even to Fred. von Schlegel.* Recently the late Prof. Max Müller came to realise it in a fashion, in so far as he recognised the one fundamental basis of all the schools of Hindu Philosophy. He says:—

"The longer I have studied the various systems, the more have I become impressed with the truth of the view taken by Vijñâna-Bhikṣhu and others that there is behind the variety of the six systems a common fund of what may be called national or popular philosophy, a large Mânasa lake of philosophical thought and language, far away in the distant North, and in the distant Past, from which each thinker was allowed to draw for his own purposes."†

While thus the idea is not entirely unknown among European scholars of Sanskrit, there has been no adequate attempt made, so far as I know, by any writer to show how exactly, if at all, the different systems can constitute a single and gradually advancing series, or how the Hindus can at all justify their position. Yet

---

* Schlegel, *Phil. of Hist.*, pp. 202 and 203.

† *Six Systems*, p. xvii.

the Hindus maintain that it *can* be justified, and that the view they hold of their Philosophy is not only correct, but is most essential to a proper understanding of their various systems.

Leaving aside, for future consideration, this claim of the Hindus and taking the position for granted, let us now see what the three standards really are.

(*b*)—THE THREE STANDARDS.

The Sanskrit word for what I have called a Standard of Philosophy is Prasthâna. Literally translated it means a setting forth, or a setting out. It may also be rendered as a standpoint or road. And, as stated above, there are three and only three standards or Prasthânas.

The Creationist or Realistic Standard.

The first standard is meant either for absolute beginners, that is to say, for students with an intelligent, but as yet philosophically unreflecting, or at any rate not much reflecting, mind; or for those otherwise unable or unwilling to study any but the *practical* truths of metaphysical Philosophy.* This standard takes up the Universe as it appears to such a mind, that is to say, as it is found extended in space and changing in time, with all the objects in it as real things and all the qualities of these objects as inherent in them and not as something subjective, existing merely in the mind of the percipient. It excludes, of course, anything of the nature of what may be called the psycho-dynamism or polyonymism† of the other two standards and has certainly nothing to do with idealism. It is naïve realism, pure and simple. As Realism, this standard has reduced the infinite

* Cha. Kâ., Vol. I, p. 115; Roer, p. xvi (implied only). † *See* Appendix B.

complexity of things to nine classes of ultimate Realities. The reduction of the infinite variety of existing and experienced things to these nine classes may be called the analysis or analytic aspect of the Universe from this standpoint.

Then, what may be called the synthetic aspect of the Universe, as taught in this standard, shows how, out of these nine classes of ultimate Realities, everything that we experience in the Universe is formed. These things, which are thus formed out of the ultimate Realities, are considered as absolutely *new* productions. They are no doubt produced out of certain ingredients which have existed from all eternity; but, before their production, they have no sort of existence whatever. They might be spoken of as absolute creations, if it were not for the fact that they are produced, not out of nothing, but out of things which have been eternally existing. And this is a point which should be borne clearly in mind; for it is with reference to this idea, that the standard takes its name, which, in Sanskrit, is Ârambha-vâda or Asat-kârya-vâda. The first of these two names can be translated as 'the doctrine of an absolutely new creation' out of pre-existing ingredients; while the second means 'the doctrine of absolute non-existence of the produced' before their actual production. For the sake of convenience we shall call it the 'creationist standard' or standpoint, bearing always in mind, that creation in this connection means, not the creating of things out of nothing, but only forming and fashioning them out of previously existing factors.

As suggested before, there are three main and original schools, started by Ṛiṣhis, which belong to this standard or standpoint.* Of these, the Dharma-mîmâṁsâ belongs to it only in so far as it has a metaphysical basis and a metaphysical conception of the origin of things; otherwise it deals chiefly with certain propositions laid down in regard to men's duties. The second school belonging to it, that is, the Nyâya, takes practically for granted several of the metaphysical doctrines, which are special to the standard, and then devotes itself very largely to the discussion of the proper means of arriving at truth, in so far as this means consists of *reasoning.*† While the third school of this standard, the Vaisheṣhika, deals chiefly with the metaphysical doctrines themselves. Thus, while the two first-named schools may be spoken of as rather practical, the third is, in a sense, more theoretical; and as my object here is to deal chiefly with the theoretical doctrines, I shall often refer to this standard by the name of its third representative, namely, Vaisheṣhika, except when there will be occasion specially to mention the other members.

I shall also speak of it as Realism, Realistic Standard, and so on.

The psycho-dynamic standard.

The second standard takes up the analysis of the Universe at the point where it was left by the Vaisheṣhika, and carries it further. It reduces the nine ultimate Realities, or entities of the Realistic System, to only two. It does not discard the nine Realities altogether but only shows that they are not final. It accepts them as

* Ad. Br, Sid., p. 51 and *passim*; Pra, Bhe., p. 23. † *Infra* pp. 138-139,

facts but points out that they are not primary but are derived from still simpler principles.* That is to say, it does with the Realities of the first standard, very much what the latest physical researches in the West are said to be doing with the atoms of matter with which Western chemistry deals. The tendency of these researches has been, as is well-known, to show that the atoms of chemistry are not ultimate Realities, but that they are derived from sources that are more simple and more universal. But while they are tending in this direction, they have not in any way interfered with the existence of atoms as definite units, albeit they are not final Realities.

The reduction of the nine Realities of the first standard to what are regarded as the two ultimate principles may be called the analytic aspect of the Universe, as held by the second standard, corresponding to the analytic aspect of the former. The second standard also possesses a synthetic aspect which in all essentials is exactly the same as that of the first, only it shows, as is natural, that the derived things are produced not from the nine Realities but from the two which it considers ultimate. Of course, it presents the synthetic aspect in greater detail and in a somewhat fuller form.

It shows how one of the two classes of ultimate Realities remains for ever unaffected and unchanged while out of the other is produced everything which can ever form an object of experience. It shows also how out of this Reality are first produced all those things or facts which are regarded as mental or psychical, such

---

* Ani., vi. 13. *See* Note 6.

as thoughts, ideas, feelings, and so on, and then out of these again everything material.

There has been much confusion in the West as to the exact nature of this standard. It derives the material from the mental and psychical, that is to say, from things which are of the nature of thoughts, ideas, and feelings. But, in spite of this fact, Prof. Garbe, who is perhaps the one scholar in the West who has made a thorough study of the literature of this standard, has yet taken it to be a form of materialism; so much so, that he has seen no place for psychology in this standard and has substituted a physiology in its stead.* This is indeed strange not only because it is absolutely against the universal tradition of the Hindus, but also because it is absurd to call a system of Philosophy materialistic which derives matter from thoughts and ideas. Prof. Max Müller, however, who generally had a better insight into things Hindu came to form a clearer and more correct conclusion as to the nature of the standard. For he recognised in it a system of idealism; and if a system that derives matter from things mental can be called idealism, it undoubtedly is so. But more properly perhaps it may be spoken of as a psycho-dynamism, inasmuch as the principles which it regards as the origin of things are both psychical, *i.e.*, of the nature of feelings, thoughts and ideas, and dynamic, *i.e.*, of the nature of forces or powers.

Being a system of psycho-dynamism it discards the creationist notion of the Vaisheṣhika, and shows that

---

* Garbe, *Sâmkh. Phil.*, p. 242 *et seq.*

† *Six Systems*, p. x.

things are not formed out of pre-existing materials, as absolutely *new* creations, but that products *already* exist in a potential form in the original psycho-dynamic principle. They simply unroll themselves out from this potential state as a tree unrolls itself out from the seed. That is to say, from this point of view, things are not created but evolved; and what is evolved already exists in a potential state. Therefore it is called Pariṇâma-vâda. This may be translated as the doctrine of evolution; and the standard may be called the evolutionist standard. It is also called Sat-kârya-vâda, that is to say, the doctrine of the existence of the product in a potential form prior to its actual manifestation.

There are, as mentioned before, two main schools, founded by Ṛiṣhis, belonging to this standard; namely,

(1) Sâṅkhya

and

(2) Yoga.

The Sâṅkhya devotes itself chiefly to the exposition of the doctrines of the standard while the Yoga occupies itself mostly with the consideration of the *practical* method by which the truths of the doctrines can be realised as direct experiences. I shall, therefore, refer to this standard as Sâṅkhya, mentioning Yoga only where it is necessary.

The polyonymic Standard.

The final standard takes up the analysis of the Universe at the point at which it was left by the evolutionist standard; and reduces the two Realities of the latter to one absolute Reality only. Like the second in its dealings with the first, the third or final standard does not entirely discard the findings of the second; only it shows how one of the two Realities recognised by the Sâṅkhya cannot be absolutely real, but that it is a something which, while it is real from one point of view, is for ever non-existent when looked at from another.

This is what it gives as the analytic aspect of the Universe; but it presents a synthetic aspect too, which is practically the same as that taught in the other standards, with such differences only as follow inevitably from the analytic view it presents.

As the Reality it teaches is absolutely unchangeable, this standard shows how the Universe, with its infinite variety, is and must be but an appearance, namely, of mere 'names and forms,' *i.e.*, concepts as such and concepts objectified. That is to say, it shows how it is one and the same thing which, remaining what it is, yet appears as many, under *many names* and concepts It may, therefore, be called a standard of polyonymism. In Sanskrit it is called Vivarta-vâda, that is to say, the doctrine of production in which the originating Reality remains what it is and yet brings about the result. It is also called Sat-kâraṇa-vâda,* that is to say, the doctrine of the reality of only the originating source or basis of things. We shall call it polyonymism,† as it is not exactly idealism in any Western sense of the word that I know of. The manifold of the Universe, according to this standard, no doubt consists only of ideas *as such* and ideas objectified—of "names and

---

* Ad. Br. Sid., p. 2. † *See* Appendix B.

forms" as they are called—which are, as it were, backed up and made substantial by the one and only Reality; but these ideas, while forming, from one point of view, an eternal series, are, under no circumstances, part of the one and absolute Reality. (*See*, however, Note 7, below).

It is represented, as stated above, by the Vedânta, by which name we shall refer also to this standard.

Scope and method of the presentation of Hindu Philosophy here made.

Of these three standards or systems of Hindu Philosophy, the last two only are chiefly known in the West. For this, we are greatly indebted to Sanskrit scholars. The first, as it seems to me, has received but scant attention, at any rate, much less attention than it perhaps really deserves.

It is, therefore, my purpose here to make an attempt at explaining the *main* and *original* doctrines of this hitherto neglected school of Hindu Realism in such a fashion as to make it intelligible to the Western student.

In making this attempt I shall first state the doctrines as clearly as I can and then give some of the reasonings which are adduced in their support.

REALISM.

A—The Analytic Aspect.

The Nine Realities.

From the Creationist standpoint, that which we call the Universe consists, as stated before, of nine classes of ultimate factors, with their various properties and relations. In Vaisheṣhika they are called Dravyas. We may translate the term by Realities or Entities,* but *not* by Substances, as has hitherto been done. The names of the nine classes of Realities are as follow :—

Enumeration of the principles.

(1) Four classes of minima of those things which are discrete and are perceived by the senses. Each of these minima is an eternal and changeless Reality† which has absolutely *no magnitude whatever* and is called an Aṇu, a Parimaṇḍala, or a Paramâṇu.‡ We shall refer to these minima as Paramâṇus.§

Paramâṇus have been translated as atoms, which is most misleading.‖ For atoms as conceived by Western chemistry are things with *some* magnitude, while Paramâṇus are *absolutely without any magnitude whatever* and *non-spatial.*

(2) An all-pervading Continuum, called Âkâsha, which may perhaps be translated as Ether ;¶ although, from the Creationist point of view, it does not possess

---

* *Infra.* † *Infra.*

‡ Nyâ. Sû., IV. ii. 16. Vaish. Sû., V. i. 13. ; VII. i. 20. Nyâ.-Bhâṣh., IV. ii. 23.; IV. ii. 14.

§ *See* Note 8. ‖ *See* Note 8. ¶ *Infra.*

exactly the same properties as the Ether of which modern Western Science speaks.

(3) A Reality, Power or Force,* having universal scope and operation; it relates things in regard to their activity, movement and change, as well as brings them into existence, urges them on, changes them, and finally destroys them. As it thus works change in things, it gives rise, in their percipients, to the notions of past, present, and future, of old and new. It is called Kâla in Sanskrit.

(4) A Reality, Power, or Force, having equally universal scope and operation, and holding things in their relative positions even while they are being driven on—in Sanskrit, Dik.†

(5) An infinite number of Realities in general touch, and with possibilities of a special relation, with everything in the Universe.‡ Each of these serves as the basis of consciousness and experience in an experiencing being. In Sanskrit these are called Âtmans. We may perhaps translate the term as Self-Ultimates (*not* Souls).

(6) An infinite number of Realities, which are all without any magnitude whatever,§ and serve as the means by which the Âtmans are brought into special relations with what the latter experience in succession. The technical name for one of these is Manas. There is no English word that I know of, which can express the exact technical meaning of this term. We might perhaps render it by Mind, but it would not be exact. I shall,

---

*** On the use of the word Power or Force (Shakti) in this connection, *see* Note 9.**

† *Infra.* ‡ *Infra.* § *Infra.*

therefore, leave the word untranslated. What it really and exactly means will be seen when we come to discuss the arguments that are advanced in support of its existence.

Reasoning in support of the principles.

The Realistic standard supports the existence of these Realities by its own line of reasoning, which will now be explained.

The Paramâṇus.

First, as regards the Paramâṇus.

There are certain facts which, *as facts*, are undisputed.

Reality of the Sensible.

People may dispute as to their ultimate nature, but not their existence as facts of experience. Of these, we experience some by means of the senses. These may, therefore, be called sensible experiences. Now, as such sensible experiences do undoubtedly exist, so there are and must be, other than and outside of ourselves as individual experiencers, things by which such experiences are produced. If we call these things collectively the sensible world or sensible matter, on account of our experiencing them by means of the senses, then such a sensible world does and must exist independently, and outside, of us as experiencing individuals. That such a world *seems* to exist nobody can doubt; for we all perceive it so. Only, some may, indeed do, imagine that this world as existing outside is a mere seeming. They hold that what really exists are only our own ideas and impressions, that is to say, purely subjective things; and that it is these alone which appear as the sensible world, which, therefore, has no independent existence whatever, as something *apart from* and *other than* our own experience—our own ideas and impressions. This cannot be true. There is, and must be, a sensible world which exists as something different from, and outside, our own experiences as individuals, and by which the sensible experiences we have are produced. That this is so we must admit for the following reasons:—

(*a*) It exists outside us as individuals, because,* if it did not, then the experiences of waking life would be of exactly the same nature as those dreams which are purely subjective.† For such dreams are experiences which have, outside them, no objects to which they correspond; and of which they are experiences had by the experiencer. That purely subjective dreams are without outside objects nobody will deny. But how do we know that there are no outside objects corresponding to subjective dreams? It is obvious we know this because we do not perceive them again on waking. But if our reason for believing that objects experienced in subjective dreams do not exist apart from our experience of them, is *because* they are *not* perceived as objects in waking, then it follows that what *is* experienced in waking does exist apart from our experiences. We can say that A does *not* exist, because *not* perceived as B, *only* if we know that what *is* perceived as B *does* exist.

---

* Nyâ. Sû., IV. ii. 33, 34.; Nyâ. Bhâṣh. and Nyâ. Vâr. on above.

† *See* Note 10,

In other words, we deny the existence of things perceived in subjective dreams, *because* we are *certain* of the existence of things experienced in waking, that is, by means of the senses. This being so, it is absurd to deny their existence again.

(*b*) If the sensible did not exist, subjective dreams themselves would be impossible.* Because they, like memories and imaginings, are nothing but repetitions, in various forms, of things already experienced as existing outside.

(*c*) Then again, if the sensible things did not exist apart from our ideas and experiences of them, there is no reason why we should not see them at will and continuously, just as we can have our own ideas at will and for as long as we like.† But in regard to sensible things, we find, that we perceive them only so long as they remain in relation with us.

This is so only because they exist independently of us.

(*d*) Then, there are, in regard to sensible things, what we call right perceptions and experiences as distinguished from mistaken ones and hallucinations.‡ This would be impossible if the sensible things did not exist. For we call that experience of a sensible thing right, which corresponds to

* Nyâ. Sû., IV. ii. 33, with Bhâṣh. and Vâr.

† Nyâ. Vṛi., IV. 99, (*i.e.*, IV. ii. 33.)

‡ Nyâ. Sû. with Bhâṣh. and Vâr., IV, ii. 37, generally.

what exists in its true nature as an externally existing thing, and, wrong and imaginary, that which does not so correspond.

For all these reasons, and others which might be adduced,* there exists a sensible world, which is independent of, and apart from, the subjective ideas and experiences of individual percipients.

And if it exists, it must be composed of Paramâṇus, *i.e., super-sensible* Realities without any magnitude whatever.

Difference between Hindu and Western Realism.

Unlike many, if not most, schools of Realism in the West, there is no Hindu system of realistic thought, which has ever held that the essential basis of the sensible world is a something or somethings which must have magnitude and extension. This idea, that the essences of the sensible world are extended things, has no doubt found great support, until recently, in the chemical theory of atoms regarded as "hard and solid" and absolutely simple factors. But with the gradual passing away of this theory, as it is said to be doing in consequence of the investigations of Prof. J. J. Thomson and others, perhaps there will be, in the West, many more now who will see how it is possible to be a thorough-going realist and yet maintain, as the Hindu Realists of all shades have always maintained, that the ultimate constituents of sensible things are indeed real, self-subsisting, and independent of all percipients, *but* they are not solid, hard particles with any magnitude, however small. A view, to be classed as Realism, need

* For instance, Brah. Sû, with Shâr. Bhâṣh., Shrî-Bhâṣh, &c., II. ii, 28,

perhaps have no more in it, than the simple admission that the sensible world should have some real and eternal basis or bases, producing and upholding what we perceive by the senses, and existing independently of the percipient. These bases may be *any* independent Realities, *with* or *without* magnitude. They might even be mere stimuli producing the sensible, *if* the stimuli could be things which existed by themselves, eternally and independently of all perceiving entities or of anything else. This being so, the Hindu Realist maintains, that the ultimate bases of the sensible world, and the originators of the sensible qualities are neither matter, which must have magnitude or extension like the atoms as formerly conceived by chemistry, nor even stimuli as generally understood in the West, but Realities—things that might be as well called real and independently existing Powers or Forces—which are without any magnitude whatever. And he does so for the following reasons:—*

Two classes of the Sensible.

What we have called sensible things or the sensible world may be divided into two classes, the visible and the invisible—the invisible being the vast aerial atmosphere, with whatever else it may contain in it in an invisible form; and the visible, everything else.

The sensible are discrete.

Now, all these sensible things, visible or invisible, are of limited extent, and, as such, discrete; that is to say, being of limited extent, they consist of parts which are separable from one another. That the visible things are discrete needs no argument. That the invisible aerial

---

* *See* Note 11.

atmosphere also is limited in extent, and consists of discrete parts, is now well-known in the West.

The Hindus established this idea by pointing to the fact that there are movements in the air, whirlwinds and so on.* These phenomena would not be possible, if the aerial atmosphere were an all-filling Reality, that is, an absolute Continuum, and were not composed of discrete parts. If a thing be an all-filling Continuum, no parts of it can possibly move away from their places nor can other parts come in from some other quarter. Nor can it have expansion, contraction or undulation or any other form of motion, all of which phenomena imply displacement of parts. If, therefore, the aerial atmosphere were an all-filling Continuum, that is to say, if it were not composed of movable parts, there could be no commotion in it. But we know there are such commotions of the atmosphere, as in storms, cyclones and so on. Therefore it must also be of limited magnitude and composed of parts.

Thus, all sensible things are of limited extent, and as such discrete, that is, consisting of parts. On account of this fact, it may be laid down as a general principle, that—

Things of limited extent must consist of parts.

How things of limited magnitude are produced.

The next point to consider is, that a discrete thing of limited magnitude can be produced in three different ways :†—

(*a*) By the addition of things having magnitudes.

---

* **Vaish. Sû., II. i. 14.**

† **Nyâ. Vâr., III. i. 33.; Upask., VII. ii. 9.**

(*b*) By the expansion or contraction of a thing of another magnitude ; and finally

(*c*) By a *number* of things standing, *not contiguously,* but at suitable distances from one another, and then entering into a combination of unification, so as to form a single unit, which, as a whole, may behave as one individual, and in which the originating parts are no longer entirely independent of the whole. In this case the originating parts or factors need not have any magnitude whatever.

As for examples of the first two cases, they are quite obvious. But in regard to the third, some explanation is needed.

Secondary units or organic wholes, (Avayavins).

First of all, we must admit that there is a great difference between a *mere aggregate,* as that of a number of atoms of Hydrogen and Oxygen, or of a number of living cells put together anyhow, and a *unified whole* such as the atoms of Hydrogen and Oxygen make when combined as water, or a single living organism like some animal body.* The unified wholes, which we may call *secondary or produced units or individuals,* behave as a single thing ; but this cannot be said to be the case in a mere aggregate of atoms or of cells. The secondary unit is a *new* thing, quite other than, and different from, the mere aggregate. We cannot deny the existence of such secondary units or produced individuals (Avayavins).

* Nyâ. Sû., II. i.; Nyâ. Bhâşh., 34-36; Nyâ. Vâr., IV. ii. 3-14 (generally).

Secondly, we know, that sensible things of limited magnitude are never absolutely solid.* On the contrary, they are and must be, porous ; otherwise 'they could not be operated upon by heat,'† which, in order to transform a thing completely as it can do, must enter into every part of it. This entire transformation of a thing would be impossible if there were any parts of the thing, *as* that thing, which were absolutely solid, as such a part would resist penetration by heat.

Porosity of the discrete sensible.

We also know that things can be compressed.

This again would be impossible if they were absolutely solid.

We must, therefore, admit that sensible things are porous. That is to say, they are composed of ultimate parts which are not absolutely contiguous, but have spaces between them.

These facts, then, may be laid down as two of the most fundamental principles in regard to the composition of sensible things of limited magnitude, namely :—

Principles governing the structure of the secondary unit or Avayavin.

(1) A number of separate things can produce a single unit or a secondary individual which is other than, and different from, a mere aggregate. And they do it by a process of unification which is and must be different from that of mere combination ; and,

(2) The ultimate particles of any thing, so produced, as *particles* of *that* thing, stand, not contiguously, but apart from one another.

---

* N. V. T. Ṭ., p. 355, lines 3 *et seq.*

† Nyâ. Mañj., p. 438 (lines 6 *et seq.*, from bottom).

Applying these principles, we can see how things of no magnitude can produce a single thing, *i.e.*, a secondary unit, of limited magnitude.

Production of things with magnitude by things of no magnitude.

First,* we can see how a thing, which is a *single* unit, having magnitude, that is to say, some length, breadth and thickness, however minute, can be produced by a *number*, which must not be *less than three*, of other things of the nature of pure lines, that is, having only length.†

Let three things of the nature of lines stand, not contiguously, in which case they will produce only a line, nor in the same plane, but apart from one another, and on two planes, say as—

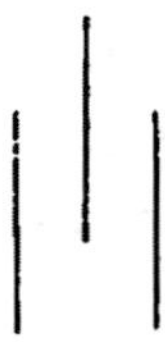

Then let them combine by the process of unification. They will then produce the single unit,

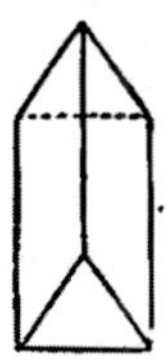

A,

that is to say, the prism A, which will be a thing with magnitude.

Next we can see how each of the lines producing the prism A can itself, as a single unit, be produced, in the same way, by a *number*, not *less than two*, of things of

* See Note 11. † See Note 12.

the nature of pure points, that is to say, without any magnitude whatever—without any length, breadth or thickness.*

Let two things of the nature of points stand, not contiguously, in which case they will produce only a point, but apart from one another, as—

. .

and then let them combine by the process of unification.

As a result of this combination we shall get the single unit

——A,

which, as a single unit, will be a thing of the nature of a pure line.

Thus, we find how things of the nature of pure points can produce things of the nature of pure lines; and these latter again, things having magnitude. That is to say, we see how things of *no magnitude* can produce things *with magnitudes.*

And this is the third way of producing things having magnitude.

The other two ways, as we have seen, are processes whereby things with magnitude are produced by things *already having magnitude.*

Things like points as the simplest of factors. These are Paramāṇus.

Finally, as things of no magnitude, *i.e.*, of the nature of points, are the simplest and cannot be conceived as consisting of any component parts, we must hold that they cannot be produced. Therefore, if they exist, they must exist eternally; for, being unproduced, they cannot be destroyed either, destruction meaning

* See Note 12.

division into component parts.* These things are called Paramâṇus.

We have said that, *if* they exist, then Paramâṇus must be eternal, as they cannot be conceived as being produced, and, therefore, as capable of destruction.† The next point we have to consider is that they *do* and must exist; and that they alone are the bases and originating ingredients of all sensible things which are discrete.

How Paramâṇus must exist and are the ultimate constituents of the discrete sensible.

For we have seen that all sensible things which are discrete are composed of parts; and as they are composed of parts, these parts must ultimately be no other than the Paramâṇus. For there is no reason to suppose that the ultimate parts must be things of some magnitude, however minute—of some length, breadth and thickness. It would indeed be necessary to stop at parts having some magnitude, however minute, and regard them as ultimate, *if* we saw no way of things with magnitude being produced by things without magnitude. But we have shown how things with magnitude can be produced from things with no magnitude. We might also stop at the smallest things having magnitude, *if* the production of these, from things without magnitude, were in violation of any of the principles which rule the production of other single units. But we have seen, that not only is there no violation of such principles, but it is by virtue of those very principles that things without magnitude can possibly produce things with magnitude.

* *See* Note 13. † *See* Note 13.

On the contrary, if there is any violation of principles, and arbitrariness, even inconsistency, anywhere, it is to be found, not in the idea of Paramâṇus, but in the view which regards the ultimate constituents of the sensible and discrete things as particles *with* magnitude.

Such particles are a violation of a principle, inasmuch as they, being of limited magnitude, are yet considered unbreakable into simpler parts; while all other sensible things having also limited magnitude are recognised as produced and capable of being broken up into simpler components.*

Then, they cannot be considered to be the simplest things, as they consist of surfaces, lines and points.

Finally, if the ultimate constituents of sensible things were composed of solid, hard and extended particles with magnitude, however small, then Âkâsha or Ether could not really be all-pervading as we shall see it must be.†

For all these reasons, we must conclude that the ultimate factors of the discrete things of sense-perception are of the measure of pure points, without any magnitude whatever, that is, without any length, breadth or thickness. They are in other words Paramâṇus.

Paramâṇus are super-sensible.

As they are without any magnitude whatever, the Paramâṇus, as such, can never be perceived by the senses.‡ They are, therefore, super-sensible or transcendental (Atîndriya). They are super-sensible, *not* in the sense that, while they are

---

* Nyâ. Vâr., II. i. 33, p. 234, line 3, &c.; N. V. T. Ṭ., p. 272, lines 3, 4. Saptap. Mit., p. 14, lines 1-3. Ki. Va. on Pṛithivî, showing how Trasareṇu cannot be final. *See* Note 14.

† *See* Note 15. ‡ Nyâ. Sû., Nyâ. Bhâṣh., Nyâ. Vâr.—IV. ii. 14.

too small to be perceived by the unassisted senses, or with the aid of any instruments which have been so far invented, they could be perceived by the senses if we had, let us say, ideally perfect instruments to aid us in our sense-observation. They are super-sensible, rather, in the sense, that they can *never* be perceived by the senses, *not* even with the aid of the most perfect instruments imaginable. That is to say, they lie altogether beyond the range of the senses and are transcendental. They are beyond the range of the senses in the same sense as colour is beyond the range of hearing, or sound, of sight. They can be conceived only by the Mind.*

Paramâṇus are non-spatial.

As Realities without any magnitude, the Paramâṇus must also be non-spatial.† That is to say, they themselves cannot occupy space or localised position (Pradeshâtîta).

No distinction in Paramâṇus in regard to measure of any kind. How they can be classified.

Being super-sensible and non-spatial entities, they are incapable of any distinction from one another in regard to size, shape, weight, density or any other form of measure. They can, therefore, never be classified with reference to any of these standards. But they are not incapable of classification. They can be classified with reference to certain qualities which they produce in the different forms of sensible things that are themselves the products of Paramâṇus.

If all sensible things of limited magnitude are produced by the Paramâṇus, as they must be, then it

* N. V. T. Ṭ., p. 271, line 7 (from bottom.)

† Nyâ. Vâr., IV. ii. 25. (p. 522, line 3); Shâr. Bhâṣh., II, ii. 12.

is obvious that the properties, which sensible things possess, are also produced by them, and are inherent in the things themselves.

Qualities inherent in things.

For, if external things exist, as they must exist, independently of the percipient,* then it is unreasonable to say, that their properties do not inhere in them but in the percipients; or that only some of the properties are inherent in them, while others are purely subjective.† For, it can be shown that the very arguments, which will prove that some of the properties are objective, will also prove that the rest are equally so. Granting that the external and sensible world exists, we cannot consistently maintain that any of its properties are subjective.‡ At best we can say that our perceptions of the properties are mere copies, perhaps very imperfect copies. But copies always imply originals. Therefore, we must admit that if the sensible world exists independently of the percipient, it has also properties which are inherent in it.

General qualities of matter.

Of these properties, there are some which are never absent from anyone of the sensible things—impenetrability, for instance. It is impossible to conceive any of the perceptible things as entirely devoid of these, unless they be hallucinations, and therefore entirely subjective. These may be and are, indeed, called the '*general properties*' (Sâmânya Guṇas) of sensible things. One distinguishing feature

---

* Vaish. Sû., II. ii. 26.

† Prashasta, p. 58, on sound as an objective quality. But this argument applies to all qualities of matter. Prashasta, p. 96.

‡ Bradley, *App. and R.*, pp. 15-17, together with *infra*, p. 36.

they all have in common is, that they can be perceived by more senses than one. Also, in regard to masses of things, they differ only in degree but not in kind. One mass is more impenetrable than another, more easily ponderable than another, softer or harder than another, and so on. They correspond to a certain extent to what are called, in modern European Philosophy, since the days of Locke, the Primary qualities of matter. We shall refer to them simply as 'general qualities.'

Special qualities of matter.

As distinguished from these, there are certain other properties, which can each be perceived by a single sense only;* and they differ, in *masses of things*, not in degree only, but in kind. That is to say, they are essentially different from one another. They form part of those qualities which are called the 'special qualities' in the Vaisheṣhika, and correspond to some of the secondary qualities mentioned in Western Philosophy. They are only four in number, namely:—

(1) Odour,
(2) Flavour,
(3) Luminosity (colour),
and
(4) Temperature (Sparsha).†

It will be noticed that one quality, namely Sound, which is also perceived by a single and special sense, has been left out of consideration here. For reasons to be explained later,‡ Sound cannot be regarded as a property of the discrete sensible things. For our

* Nyâ. Bhâṣh., III. i. 56 and 57.

† Prashasta, p. 106. Kandalî on same, *See* Note 16.

‡ *Infra*.

present purpose it will be quite sufficient to say that there is no discrete sensible thing from which Sound cannot be entirely eliminated; that is to say, which cannot be conceived as absolutely silent. Sound can no doubt be produced by means of every one of the sensible forms of things, and may, for this reason and in this sense, be said to be common to them all; but at the same time there is no sensible thing, which cannot exist without it.

However this may be, there is one feature which is common to Sound as well as to the four properties named above, namely, that they are each perceived by a single and special sense only. They, in this respect, differ from the above-mentioned general or primary properties, and may, as distinguished from the latter, be, and indeed they are, called the 'special properties' of the sensible. They correspond, it is obvious, to the secondary qualities of Locke and modern European Philosophy. We shall refer to them as Special Qualities.

Of the five special qualities belonging to the sensible world, Sound, for the reason just hinted at, need not be taken into consideration now. In regard to the remaining four, it is obvious that they are all essentially different from one another. We cannot speak of flavour as being only a higher or lower degree of odour; of odour as only colour in a different degree; or of temperature as colour in a varying grade.

Nor will it do to say that these qualities are purely subjective,* that is, they exist in the percipient only

* *Infra.*

and not in the things perceived, and that the primary qualities alone are inherent in matter. For, as stated before, this position is untenable. If some are regarded as objective, the rest can also be shown to be exactly on the same footing, and by the same line of reasoning; or if some are thought to be subjective, the rest must also share the same fate for exactly the same reasons.* This latter position, however, of regarding every property of the sensible world, as subjective, can be held only by an Idealist Philosopher, because he denies the existence of an external world, independent of, and apart from, thoughts and ideas which are regarded as part and parcel of an experiencing subject or subjects. But as, for reasons stated before, this view of an external and sensible world not existing independently nf and apart from an experiencer or experiencers, cannot be accepted as valid, and, as an alternative, we must admit the existence of the sensible, we must also admit that the secondary or special qualities are as objective as the primary or general ones. The four qualities, therefore, mentioned above must be held as objective, and inherent in the things perceived.

Classification of the Paramâṇus with reference to the special properties of matter.

Of these two classes of properties of sensible things, the Paramâṇus can be classified, only with reference to the four special qualities which differ from one another not merely in degree but essentially; and which, unlike the general qualities, are not all present in everything sensible. And the way

---

* Bradley, *App. and R.*, pp. 15-17.

to classify the Paramâṇus with reference to these qualities is as follows :—

Classification of sensible matter.

It is well known that there are many things from which odour can never be eliminated as long as they exist as those things and do not change into some other things which are essentially different.* It belongs to their very essence. While, as a distinctive quality, it is inalienable from this class of things, it is not essential to many others, from which it can be easily eliminated. We might take our example of this class of things indifferently from what are called chemical elements or from other 'compounds.' For from the standpoint of Hindu Philosophy they are *all* compounds—both the chemical elements as well as what are regarded as products of the latter. For chemical atoms of elements, as well as other things, are of limited magnitude. And nothing that has any magnitude whatever, excepting infinite magnitude, can be simple. Thus while we might point to anything having inalienable odour as an example of this class, I shall simply mention such a thing as 'musk.' This substance can never be imagined as without odour, as long as it remains 'musk,' while the pure aerial atmosphere, or absolutely pure water, need not have any odour at all.

Then again, there are things from which flavour can never be absolutely eliminated,† (so long as they remain as those things in regard to their essential formation), while it is not so inalienable in the case of many others. There are, for instance, many juicy things which are

---

* Lakṣh. on Pṛithivî, p. 1. † *See* Note 17.

never without flavour, while the pure air of our previous example is flavourless.

Similarly, it is inconceivable that the substance of the sun and the stars can be absolutely without luminosity, unless it undergoes complete change and transformation.* Luminosity or colour is of the very essence of such substances, while there are many other things which have no such inalienable self-luminous property.

Finally, while odour, flavour and luminosity are each inalienable in one or other form of matter, they are entirely accidental to pure air. While pure air can be easily divested of odour and flavour, and is colourless, that is, without self-luminosity, it is inconceivable without temperature.† Temperature belongs to its very essence.

There is, as stated before, no form of sensible matter with which Sound is for ever and inalienably present. Sound can no doubt be produced by all forms of sensible matter. But it is not inalienably, and always, present with any, as the four other qualities are.

Thus we find that all sensible and compound matter, with reference to the four inalienable qualities, can be divided into four great classes.

(1) That form of sensible and compound matter from which all other special qualities, such as odour, flavour and colour can be eliminated, but not temperature, which is essential to it.

(2) That from which luminosity can never be eliminated and to which it is essential.

(3) That from which flavour cannot be eliminated, and to which it is essential.

*** Lakṣh. on Tejaḥ, p. 4.** **† Lakṣh. on Vâyu, p. 6.**

(4) That from which odour can never be eliminated and to which it is essential.

Of course, this does not mean that compounds of succeeding classes do not possess the essential and inalienable qualities of the preceding ones.* They may, and indeed do, possess them. Thus, for instance, things of the fourth class have always some temperature while they can certainly be visible, *i.e.*, can have colour or luminosity, and can be tasted under suitable conditions. What is meant by classifying them in the above fashion is, that in each class there is only one special quality which is inalienable, and that the class possesses it, either as the sole special quality (as in the first), or as a quality which, being inalienable, is also peculiar to the class (as in the remaining three).

Technical and symbolical names of the four classes of sensible matter.

Of these four classes, the first is to be found most abundantly, as is evident, in the atmosphere of pure air. This class of sensible matter (compound and produced matter, of course, and not a chemical element) is therefore *technically* and *symbolically* called Air (Vâyu), *meaning* thereby only a form of matter from which all other sensible special qualities can be eliminated, but not temperature.

The second class is met with most abundantly in the fiery substance of the sun and stars. It is therefore technically and symbolically called Fire (Tejaḥ).

As the flavour of a really objective thing is had only when it is dissolved into a liquid or *watery* form,—if

---

* Vaish. Sû., II. i.1-4 ; Nyâ. Sû., III. i. 61 and 62.

it is not already so,—the third class of sensible matter is technically and symbolically called Water (Ap.)

Finally, the solid earth, with all its various flowers, fruits, vapours and so on, being a great storehouse of things to which odour is both essential and distinctive, the fourth class is technically and symbolically called Earth (Pṛithivî).

We may perhaps retain the original Sanskrit terms for these four classes of sensible matter. But if their English equivalents must be used, then they may perhaps be translated as follows:—

(1) Thermal matter;
(2) Self-luminous matter;
(3) Flavoury matter; and
(4) Odoriferous matter.

Misunderstanding in regard to Hindu conception of sensible matter.

As there has been much misunderstanding in the West as to the exact notion which the Hindus have in regard to these four classes of *extended* matter, (the misunderstanding being greatly due to the mistranslation, by the word elements, of the general name which is given to them, namely, Bhûtas), it may be well to emphasise here that they are all *compound* and *produced* forms of matter. The Hindus *never* looked upon any of these as an indivisible substance, or as *elements* in the Western chemical sense of the word. The Paramâṇus are the only indivisible elements, if elements they must be called, by which the four classes of discrete sensible matter, having limited magnitude, are produced.

And, as these are the only forms of sensible matter of limited magnitude, and as there are no others, which can be distinguished from them by any other special and essentially different characteristic which is peculiar to itself, it must be held that the Paramâṇus themselves, out of which the four classes of sensible matter are produced, are also of four, and only four, classes.*

How Paramâṇus must also be of four classes.

How this is so can perhaps be illustrated as follows: Suppose there are only four spectra of colours. Of these, let us suppose again, the first three, in addition to other colours, contain respectively bands of black, of red and of blue as their essential and distinctive features, and the fourth contains nothing but yellow. Then suppose, that these four are colours which are essentially different from one another, so that none can be derived from the others; and finally, that there are no other *kinds* of essentially different colours in any of the four spectra. Such a group of spectra can be possible, only if there are four essentially different classes or types of factors, (vibrations or stimuli as they would be called in this case), which can originate such essentially different colours. Similarly, it must be admitted that the Paramâṇus, which produce the four special and essentially different qualities in sensible matter, are and can be of four classes only. They may be named as follows:—

(1) The Paramâṇus producing inalienable temperature but no other special qualities.

(2) Paramâṇus producing inalienable colour, or luminosity, (with some temperature, of course, because

---

* *See* Note 18.

all luminous things must have some sort of temperature).

(3) Paramâṇus producing inalienable flavour (with some temperature, and colour, *i.e.* visibility under suitable conditions).

(4) Paramâṇus producing inalienable odour (with some temperature and colour and flavour, *i.e.*, visibility and tastability under suitable conditions).

Or, with reference to the particular classes of sensible things themselves, they are spoken of as:—

(1) The Vâyu-Paramâṇus, which enter into the composition of, and originate temperature in Vâyu or the aerial atmosphere.

(2) The Tejaḥ-Paramâṇus, which originate luminosity in all self-luminous things.

(3) The Ap-Paramâṇus, which originate flavour in all compounds which have only flavour but no odour.

(4) The Pṛithivî-Paramâṇus, which originate odour in compounds having odour.

What is really different in different classes of Paramâṇus.

These different classes of Paramâṇus are different from one another, it may be repeated, not in weight or any other *measure*, but only in their *capacity* to produce the four special qualities in those various sensible things which are of limited magnitude and which, as such, are themselves but Paramâṇus in compound forms. In fact the four classes of Paramâṇus are even what may be called Forces, Powers or Stimuli which produce all that affects our senses as things of limited magnitude possessing, among others, the four special properties of temperature, and so on. Only, the Paramâṇus are things which are real because they are self-subsisting and cannot be conceived as originating from something else. They are real and self-subsisting Forces or Stimuli—if one may call them so. It may also be repeated that while, as compounds, the Paramâṇus produce things of limited magnitude and their qualities affecting our senses, they themselves, *i e.*, as simple and uncompounded factors, are for ever super-sensible, as they must be, on account of their having no magnitude whatever.

No sub-classes in Paramâṇus.

It might perhaps be said here that, if the Paramâṇus can be divided into four classes with reference to the four special qualities they originate,* they can also be considered as having a much larger variety on account of the varieties which there are in each of the four special qualities themselves.† This would indeed be so, if the varieties of a special quality were different *essentially* from one another. But they are not. Indeed, that they are but *varieties* of *one* special quality, points to the fact that they must all have a single common basis, just as the varieties of colour in the solar spectrum have one common source which is the light of the sun. Moreover, we see that the same temperature, colour, flavour and odour may appear as a different shade or variety, either to the same person under different conditions, or to different persons under the same conditions. But a colour can never lose its character as colour to be perceived as temperature or as flavour. And this is so, because while temperature, colour, flavour and odour are different from one another

* Nya. Vâr., III. i. 4, (p. 355, lines 2 *et seq*.

† N. V. T. Ṭ., pp. 254, 355 beginning line 3 from bottom of p. 354.

in essence, different shades or varieties of one and the same special quality are but the results of one and the same *kind* of essential factors, that is, Paramâṇus.

There are, therefore, only four classes of Paramâṇus; and each of the four classes is, in itself, entirely without any other variety. Each of them may be said to be the *general form* of all the varieties of a single class. There are, in other words, no minor divisions or classes in a general class of Paramâṇus.

How Paramâṇus originate the corresponding senses.

Finally, each of the four classes of Paramâṇus, as the origin of a special quality perceived by a single special sense, is also the origin of the particular sense itself.* That is to say, the four classes of Paramâṇus produce respectively:—

(i) The Temperature-Sense,†
(ii) Sight,
(iii) Taste, and
(iv) Smell.

That they do so may be supported by the following arguments:—

Each of the special senses reveals to us only a single quality and none other.‡ And it reveals to us only that quality which it can itself produce, that is to say, which it possesses as a capacity and in a pre-eminent degree. That a special sense, revealing a single quality, has that quality as a capacity in abundance, or, which is the same thing, has the capacity of producing that quality, can be very easily ascertained by exciting the various sense-organs. Thus, for instance, excitations of the optic

* Vaish. Sû., VIII. ii. 5 and 6. Nyâ. Sû., I. i. 14; III. i. 60, 68, 69 and 70. Upask., VIII. ii. 5.

† *See* Note 19.

‡ Upask., VIII. (II. 5, p. 371, line 5).

nerve by artificial means will produce colour, that is to say, a form of luminosity. But the capacity to produce a particular special quality on the part of a thing, simply means that the latter is made up of Paramâṇus of a particular kind. For it is only the Paramâṇus of a particular class which alone, as we have seen, constitute the capacity to produce a special quality of a particular kind. Therefore, a special sense, having the capacity to produce a single special quality, and thus revealing exclusively that quality, must be made up of Paramâṇus which alone constitute such a capacity.

Thus it is established that the four senses, namely,

(i) The Temperature-sense,
(ii) Sight,
(iii) Taste, and
(iv) Smell,

are made up respectively of Paramâṇus producing in the sensible

(i) Temperature,
(ii) Luminosity,
(iii) Flavour, and
(iv) Odour.

The above argument is given almost in the very words of the old Nyâya and Vaisheṣhika works. But the idea is really very simple. It is only this:—

The special senses are essentially of the same nature as the essential ingredients or originators of the qualities themselves. And the truth and justice of this idea will be at once apparent, if we substitute for Paramâṇus, special kinds of stimuli; and regard them as real facts of nature, corresponding to the excitations in ourselves.

If it is true that there are different kinds of stimuli in nature for the different sensations produced in us, and that these sensations are so produced by *corresponding* excitations of our nervous system, there is also truth in the Nyâya-Vaisheṣhika idea that the senses in man are essentially of the same nature as the essential ingredients or originators of the qualities which are perceived by means of them.

Paramâṇus produce the discrete sensible.

Thus, we find, that all objects of limited magnitude in the sensible world, with their various qualities, as well as the four special senses by which we perceive them, are produced by the Paramâṇus, which are the essential Realities in them.

The sense of hearing by which sound is perceived and the faculties of touching and handling and so on, which constitute the other characteristics of living bodies, have been left out of consideration here. What they are and how they are produced, according to the Nyâya-Vaisheṣhika, will be seen later on.

So far, then, with regard to the Paramâṇus, or the first four classes of ultimate Realities, which are taught by the Realistic system.

The Âkâsha.

The existence of the fifth Reality (Âkâsha) is maintained on the following grounds* :—

A medium of connection between the discrete wanted.

The Paramâṇus are like pure points. We have seen that they produce things of limited magnitude; but they cannot do so if they actually touch one another. For in that case they can only produce

* *See* Note 20.

points. They produce things by standing away from one another and yet being joined. That is to say, they unite not contiguously but mediately. And as they are joined together mediately, there must be some Reality which, being in touch with different Paramâṇus which are otherwise separate from one another, serves as a medium for their union.*

The medium must be a continuum. It is Âkâsha.

This medium of union must be a non-discrete Reality or a Continuum which is in touch with all discrete things; in other words, is all-pervading. For if it be not such, it must ultimately consist of Paramâṇus like all other discrete things;† and these Paramâṇus must be conceived as producing it only by standing at certain distances from one another.‡ But if it be produced in this way, then we shall be under the necessity of assuming that there must be some other thing, besides itself, which serves as a medium for the union of *its* Paramâṇus. In that case, this latter substance will be the all-pervading continuum. That there must be an all-pervading continuum, to serve as a medium for the union of discrete things, cannot very well be doubted. And as there is no proof of the existence of, and no reason to suppose that there exists, any other discrete form of things besides the four we have already named, we must admit that the Reality, which serves as a medium for the union of the Paramâṇus of the four sensible forms, is itself a continuum. This all-pervading continuum and universal medium of union of discrete things

---

* Nyâ. Bhâṣh., IV. ii. 21, line 15.

† Nyâ. Sû. Nyâ., Bhâṣh., IV. II. 21; Vaish. Sû., VIII. i. 22; Prashasta, p. 58, line 16. Kandalî p. 62, line 15, &c.

‡ See Note 21.

is called Âkâsha. And, as suggested before, we may perhaps translate it as Ether, bearing in mind that, from the standpoint of Hindu Realism, it does not possess exactly the same properties as those ascribed to Ether by modern Western Science.

That Âkâsha exists, we must admit, says the Vaisheṣhika, for another reason also.

We have seen, in a general way, that the quality of sound cannot be said to inhere in any of the four forms of sensible matter we have named.* It is, no doubt, produced by the movements of one or other of the four classes of sensible matter, and they may even be needed to communicate it to a perceiving being like ourselves. The Hindu says they *may* be needed for this purpose, because nobody has ever yet entered a vacuum and tried to find out whether or not sound could be communicated to us without them.† While thus the movements of the four forms of matter are necessary for its production, and perhaps for its communication, sound cannot be said to inhere in any of them: because a quality, which can be said to inhere in a discrete thing of a particular type, has the following characteristics :—

Sound is not a property of the discrete sensible.

Characteristics of special qualities inherent in the discrete sensible.

(*a*) It endures as long as the thing endures in that particular form.‡

(*b*) It can never be separated from the thing unless the latter undergoes some radical or chemical change.§

---

* Cha. Kâ., Vol. I, pp. 159 and 172-173.

† *Ibid.*

‡ Vaish. Sû., II. i. 24, 25 and 26 (implied).

§ Prashasta, p. 58, lines 8-10.

(c) It reappears in any combination, with other things, of the thing in which it inheres,—such a combination being of the nature in which its different factors can be distinguished from one another, as for instance, a mosaic.*

These wanting in sound.

None of these conditions holds good of sound in its relation to any sensible matter. (a) There is nothing in which the sound lasts as long as the thing lasts in that condition, for all sensible things can be conceived as being perfectly silent, that is, soundless.† (b) There is nothing from which sound cannot be entirely eliminated.‡ (c) And, finally, the sound produced by a thing, which is itself produced by the combination of a number of things still distinguishable from one another in the combination, is never exactly the same as the combined sounds of the parts of which the thing is composed.§ For instance, the sound produced by a violin, is absolutely different (i) from that produced by any of the separate parts of which the violin is a combination and which are still distinguished from one another in their combination as the violin; or (ii) from that which may be conceived as the combination of the separate sounds produced by the separate parts.

For all these reasons it must be admitted that sound does not inhere like temperature, colour, flavour or odour in any form of discrete sensible matter.

---

* Vivr., p. 437, lines *et seq* (implied)

† Vaish. Sû., II. i. 24-26.

‡ Prashasta, p. 58, lines 8-10.

§ V vr., p. 437, lines *et seq.*

Yet it is a quality, and as such must inhere in some Reality. For, as a quality, it can have no independent existence of its own. There is no example whatever of a quality having such an independent existence, and sound cannot be an exception to this universal rule.* Nor can it be said that it is purely subjective and inheres in the perceiving entity. For, if it were subjective and inherent in the percipient, then one would feel it to be part and parcel of oneself as, say, pain or pleasure, or a thought and an idea. But nobody feels in this way when a bell rings and he hears the sound. He does not think or feel that it is *his* sound. He rather feels that the sound proceeds from where the bell rings. Therefore, it cannot be said to inhere in the perceiving being. Moreover, all the reasons which support us in our idea that the qualities perceived by the other special senses belong, not to the percipient being, but to things other than the percipient, apply also in the case of sound. If those qualities are not inherent in the percipient, neither is sound. In this way, it can be shown that there is nothing among the otherwise known things in which sound inheres. We must, therefore, conclude that, in addition to everything else which is known otherwise, there must be some other Reality in which sound inheres; and it is this Reality which is Âkâsha. In Âkâsha all discrete things move and as they move they produce sounds not in themselves, that is, as a property inherent in themselves, but in the medium in which

Quality must inhere in reality. Sound not subjective. It inheres in Âkâsha.

---

* **Vivṛ., p. 437, lines 1, 2, 3; Vaish. Sû., II. i. 26; Prashasta, p. 58, lines 10-12.**

they move.* And it is obvious that this medium is Âkâsha which connects all discrete things.

Âkâsha is eternal.

Thus we find that Âkâsha exists, and we have already seen that it is and must be an all-pervading continuum; and being a continuum,† it must also be eternal, unproduced and indestructible. For, as mentioned before, production and destruction of a thing can only mean the bringing together of parts in a certain way, and their separation or re-arrangement,—things which are both impossible in the case of a continuum. Therefore it is eternal.

Âkâsha is motionless.

It is also absolutely motionless.‡ For, being a continuum, it cannot be conceived as moving from one place to another, nor can it contract and expand, which can mean only the bringing closer together, or throwing farther apart, of parts or particles—things which are possible only in discrete substances. Neither is there any undulatory movement in it, for that even means displacement of parts, namely, their moving up and down or back and forth.

Âkâsha is supersensible.

Finally, Âkâsha is super-sensible, as it neither is, nor can ever be, perceived by the senses.§ For everything that is perceived by the senses is so perceived by means of some contrast. Contrast, again, means some sort of distinction and isolation, neither of which is possible in regard to Âkâsha. Being a uniform continuum, (*i.e.*, not being aneka-dravya-vat), there can be no distinction made

---

* Vaish. Sû., II. i. 27; Prashasta, p. 58; lines 13 and 14.

† Vaish. Sû., II. i. 28; Prashasta, p. 68, lines 17-19.

‡ Vaish. Sû., V. ii. 21. § Vaish. Sû., IV. i. 6.; VIII. i. 6 and 7.

between different parts of itself. Similarly, being all-pervading, it can never be isolated from other things so as to enable us to distinguish it from them. Thus Âkâsha is, and must be, super-sensible.

But although itself super-sensible, its special property, sound, is perceived by means of a special sense.

The sense of hearing is only Âkâsha conditioned.

This special sense, that is, hearing, therefore, must be essentially of the same nature as Âkâsha itself ; and this for the same reasons which led us to conclude that the four other special senses are essentially of the same nature as the Paramâṇus which produce the qualities that the special senses severally reveal to us.* Only, in the case of hearing, we have to admit that it is produced not by any part of Âkâsha being actually separated off or built into something else,—for such things are impossible in the case of a continuum, —but by its being only *conditioned* in particular ways, by means of the peculiar structure of the ear. This structure, being interfered with, may make alterations in the particular *conditioning* of Âkâsha, and thus only can it be said that hearing is destroyed.

The Bhûtas or Matter.

So far, then, we find five classes of entities as eternal Realities, and therefore ultimate constituents of the Universe, namely :—

(1) Pṛithivî Paramâṇus, or odorous minima,
(2) Ap Paramâṇus, or flavour producing minima,
(3) Tejaḥ Paramâṇus, or luminous minima,
(4) Vâyu Paramâṇus, or thermal minima, and
(5) Âkâsha, ethereal continuum, or simply Ether.

---

* Nyâ. Vâr., III. ii. 72, p. 400. Nyâ. Bhâṣh., III. ii. 73, Praśhasta, pp. 58, 59.

They are all super-sensible. Only their products are sensible. That is to say, it is only the four forms of perceptible matter, with their various qualities, produced by the four classes of Paramâṇus in their various combinations, and the various sounds produced in Âkâsha, which are sensible.

These five classes are collectively called the Bhûtas.* We may translate the term as Matter, which, *as* Paramâṇus and Âkâsha, is, of course, absolutely simple and uncompounded.

Kâla and *Dik*.

Misconceptions about Kâla and Dik.

As to the next two Realities, Kâla and Dik, as taught by Hindu Realism, there has been much misconception, owing as much to confusion in regard to their real import as to the rendering, by Substance, of the word Dravya, which is given as the general name to all the nine classes of Realities. Dravya means a *something that is independently real and is self-subsisting.* Thus a Force even may be a Dravya if it can be shown to have an *independent* existence. And there is no reason why Kâla and Dik should not be Dravyas in this sense.†

Kâla.

That Kâla exists as a Reality or as an independently existing Force, is maintained by the following reasoning:—

All perceptible things are perceived as moving, changing, coming into existence and passing out of it.‡ They

* Nyâ. Sû. or Nyâ. Bhâṣh., I. i. 13. Prashasta, p. 22.

† *See* Note 22.

‡ Vaish. Sû., II. ii. 9; VII. i, 25. Prashasta, p. 25, line 10.

are produced and destroyed. There must be some Force or Power which thus brings them into existence and moves them off.* The things themselves cannot do it. If the discrete things had the power of self-origination and self-movement, then, there is no reason why there should be that mutual relation between things which persists even when they are all moving and changing or why there should be that orderly movement which there is in the Universe that we perceive.† In the Universe things are all moving in a regular and orderly fashion; they come into existence also in order, and in seasons. There must, therefore, be something which makes this orderly movement and seasonable origination and destruction of things possible.

And if it exists, it must also be conceived as having full scope and operation over all discrete things, because all discrete things are moving and changing. Âkâsha might have been this Power inasmuch as it is in touch with all discrete things; but it cannot be so, because, as we saw, Âkâsha is also the basis of a special property, namely, sound, which is produced in it the moment it comes into a special relation with discrete things.

Things with special property can affect or be affected by others only through special relations.

Now, anything which manifests a special quality can affect, or be affected by, other things, only when it comes into special relation with them, and not by a merely general relation,—that is to say, by mere aggregation or even by mere

* *See* Note 23.

† Kandalî, p. 68, lines 10 *et seq.*

contact.* Paramâṇus, for instance, are things which manifest the four special qualities named above. But they cannot do this by merely coming together, that is, by forming mere aggregates. When, however, they enter into *special relations* with one another and form compounded wholes, *i.e.*, secondary units (chemical or biological), then only do the special qualities appear. But as they can appear only when the Paramâṇus producing the secondary units affect one another, the appearance of the special qualities under the above conditions also means that the Paramâṇus as the bases of the special qualities can so affect or be affected only when they enter into *special relations*, one with the other, but not by mere aggregation.†

Similarly, we shall see‡ that Âtmans, which have also special qualities of their own, can never affect or be affected by things, unless they come into special relations with the latter; and this is so in spite of the fact that, being all-pervading entities, they are always in touch, *i.e.*, in general relation, with all things. But the moment the Âtmans enter into special relations with things and thus affect or are affected by them, there at once arise the special qualities which belong to them. It is no doubt true that some Âtmans can affect and be affected by all things. But that is so not because they are in *mere* touch with all things, but because they have that special and intimate relation with all things which other Âtmans have only with a few things.§

*** N. V. T. Ṭ., p. 280, line last but one. Ki. Va., p. 114.**

† See Note 24. **‡ *Infra*.**

§ *Infra*, pp. 86, 87 and 123 *et seq.* and Note 48.

Thus we find, first, that there is nothing which has a special quality and can yet affect or be affected by other things without entering into special relations with them. Secondly, as soon as things having special qualities enter into the various special relations with other things and thus affect or are affected by them, there at once appear, in them, those special qualities which are their own.

This being so, Âkâsha, which has a special quality of its own, cannot possibly affect all things equally by mere contact. To do so it must enter into special relations with them, and thereby have at once sound produced in it.

Therefore, if Âkâsha were that Power and Reality which affects and thereby moves on everything that is movable, it would have, in the first place, to enter into that special and intimate relation with all things, which it has now with one thing and now with another, according as the one or the other produces sound in it. Secondly, it must have this universally special relation (if such a phrase can be used) with all things, not only *occasionally*, but always; for all things, capable of movement, are moving always. Thirdly, as they move, all movements of theirs would be always producing sound. But this is never the case.

We must, therefore, conclude that, that Reality which moves all things by having a general relation with all, is something other than Âkâsha.

For similar reasons it cannot be identified with any other all-pervading Reality which has special properties and is thus capable of coming into special relations,

We must, therefore, recognise that there must be a general principle of movement, which has only a general relation with every thing that moves, comes into being, changes and passes out of existence. It is this something, this Power or Force, which is Kâla.

How and in what sense Kâla is Time.

As it moves and changes things, it gives rise in the percipient to the notions, with regard to those things, of past, present and future; of old and new.* That is to say, it produces all those relations which are termed temporal and is *in this sense only* Time.

It must be conceived as a Reality† because it cannot be shown to be dependent for its existence upon anything; rather it is upon Kâla that all moving and discrete things depend, in so far as they have movements and change.

It must be also a Reality which pervades the whole Universe; that is to say, has relation with all things that are moving and changing.‡ In fact it is a Reality which relates things together in regard to their movements and changes, and thus enables a percipient, as suggested above, to speak of some things as old, and of others as young, with reference to one another.

Dik.

The existence of the next Reality as recognised by Realism, namely, Dik or the Power, Force or Principle of relative *position*,

* Vaish. Sû., Upask., and Vivṛ., II. ii. 6. Nyâ. Vâr., II. i. 36; N. V. T. Ṭ., p. 280, &c.

† Vaish. Sû., II. ii. 7; N. V. T. Ṭ., p. 280, last line.

‡ Vaish. Sû., VII. i. 25.

which discrete things hold, is maintained in the following way* :—

Things are not only moving and changing, but they hold relative positions,† that is, stand at relative distances from one another at all moments of time. They are held together in these positions.‡ That is to say, they must be conceived as being acted upon by another Power or Force, which acts in a direction, opposite (viparîta) to that in which Kâla operates,§ and thus acting in opposition to Kâla, makes the relative position of things at any given moment of time possible. Here again the things themselves cannot thus maintain their relative positions.‖ For they are discrete and separated from one another; and unless there be something else to hold them together, there is no reason why or how they should thus retain their respective positions and positional relations to one another, while all things are moving on by virtue of Kâla. Nor can Âkâsha, although all-pervading, be the Power which keeps things in their relative positions, for exactly the same reasons for which it cannot be the all-moving Power. That is to say, it is incapable of affecting or operating on things without entering into special relations, and without thereby having sound produced in it. But the Power that can hold all things together at relative distances from one another, at any given moment of time, and can thus enable them all to retain their mutual positional relations, must be

---

* *See* Note 25. † Vaish. Sû., II. ii. 10.

‡ *Infra*. § Ki. Va., p. 144.

‖ Kandalî, p. 67, lines 19 *et seq.*

a thing which has only a general relation with all, and yet, by virtue of that relation alone, operates on them all, as it must, to keep them in positional order. Nor can Kâla be this Reality; because, as already said, the Power we are considering is a Power which acts in a way which is exactly contrary to that in which Kâla operates; and operating in opposition to Kâla makes relative position possible. We must, therefore, recognise the existence of a separate principle as the upholder of positional relations and order on the part of discrete things. This something, this Reality, Power or Force, is called Dik.

Dik produces notions of spatial directions but is not space.

As it upholds relative positions among things, it gives rise in their percipients to the notions of far and near; in this direction or in that direction; of east and west; and so on.* That is to say, it produces relations among things of the nature of what may be called spatial *directions*. But Dik cannot be called space itself, if that means place, locality or room. This latter is really Âkâsha.† It is in Âkâsha as space, *i.e.*, place or room, and as a Reality, that Dik holds things in different positions.

Difference between Âkâsha as space and Dik.

The difference between Âkâsha as space, or place, and Dik, is much the same as that between, say, a wall on which, and cords by which, pictures may be hung. The wall is or supplies the space, place or room, and the cords hold the pictures in different

* Bhâshâ Par., 45.

† *See* Notes 20 and 25; Prashasta, p. 22, line 11; Kandalî, p. 22, line 17,

positions in the space so supplied. This is a point which should be clearly borne in mind as otherwise there will be, as indeed there has been, much confusion made in regard to the meanings of Âkâsha and Dik.*

Dik is a Reality because it cannot be shown to be dependent on anything else for its existence.† It must be conceived as all-pervading, that is, having relations with all things, inasmuch as all discrete things exist in relative positions in the Universe.

Kâla and Dik uphold the Universe in Âkâsha as space.

Kâla and Dik are thus Realities which hold together the sensible Universe as, in the infinite space of Âkâsha, it ever moves on in well-regulated and seasoned cycles, and yet maintains that positional order which, for ever, obtains between its various members.‡

The Âtman.

Âtman recognised by all the systems.

The question of the existence of Âtman, that is to say, the eighth class of Realities, has been treated most elaborately. But as the Vaisheṣhika doctrine in this respect has been fairly correctly represented in the West, I shall give here only a few of the most characteristic arguments which are adduced in its support. And I shall give these not only from the Nyâya-Vaisheṣhika, but from the other systems as well; because while the various schools have had different teachings as to the nature of

* Trans. Tarkas., p. 133., para. 2

† Vaish. Sû., II. ii. 11; N. V. T. Ṭ., p. 280, last line.

‡ Prashasta, p. 22.

the Âtman, they all have alike taught its existence as an independent, eternal, and infinite Reality, lying, so to say, at the background of every experiencing entity.

In regard to the nature of the Âtman, the Creationist standard shows it to be that Reality in which consciousness or experience is only sustained, but of which experience is not an essential, an absolutely inalienable characteristic; while the Sâṅkhya reasons out that the Âtman is Feeling Intelligence itself, but teaches, in agreement with the Realistic System, that Âtmans are infinite in number. Finally, the Vedânta establishes that the Âtman is not only Intelligence itself, but it is one and the same in all experiencing beings. For these reasons, arguments in support of the Âtman, in so far as only its existence as an eternal and infinite, *i.e.*, all-reaching Reality is concerned, can be adduced from all the Standards. We may, however, begin with the following, which is perhaps the most characteristic of the Nyâya-Vaisheṣhika arguments.

Âtman *is*, because consciousness or experience as property must inhere in some Reality.

In each experiencing being there is and must be an Âtman which is an independent Reality and different from the body, because:—

(*a*) Consciousness, *i.e.*, *Experience* in general, is a property*—consciousness, namely, of things, thoughts and ideas; of feelings, pleasure, pain and so on.

(*b*) As a property it can have no independent existence of its own.†

---

* Nyâ. Sû., Nyâ. Bhâṣh., Nyâ. Vâr., I. i. 10.

† Prashasta, p. 99, lines 9 *et seq.* Kandalî on above.

There is nothing which is a property and yet has an independent existence, apart from that of which it is a property. A property must inhere in and belong to some Reality. Consciousness, as a property, must also belong to and inhere in some Reality.

(c) The materialist says it inheres in and belongs to the body. But this, for the reasons to be mentioned immediately, is impossible. Therefore, there must be some other Reality in which it inheres; and that to which it belongs is the Âtman.*

If consciousness be a reality, then it is itself the Âtman.

If it be held that consciousness is not a property, and that it is a Reality which has an independent existence, then there is hardly any need for further argument. For in that case the difference would be one of name only. In reality it will be the very thing which is called Âtman by the Hindu.†

Consciousness cannot be a property of the body.

But if it be regarded as a property, then it cannot be the property of the body, for the following reasons :—

Because, if it were a property of the body, it would exist also in the various parts of the body and ultimately in the ingredients, *i.e.*, the Bhûtas, of which it is composed, even when these were separated from one another and the body divided up. We find in a combined whole no property which cannot also be found in the

---

* *See* Note 26 for full references to authorities on the whole of this section on Âtman.

† Kandalî, p. 71, lines 17 *et seq.*
Sid. Cha., leaf 12 (second side).

parts and ingredients of which the whole is made up and into which it can be divided. But this is never the case with any part of the body nor with its ingredients, the Bhûtas. And there being no consciousness in the parts and ingredients of the body, consciousness cannot be the property of the body.

If, as an exception to this rule, it be pointed out that intoxicating power is produced by combination of ingredients which severally do not possess it, the objection can be met by saying that this is not quite a proper analogy. For the contention is not that there may not develop in a compound a new or hitherto unobserved property which has not been present in the ingredients, but that when such a compound and therewith a new property are produced, the newly produced property is always found, in howsoever small a degree, even in the smallest part, *as still a compound*, of the compounded whole. Thus, taking the very example of the objector, if intoxicating power is produced in a cask of whisky, not only was such 'power' present, though it might not have been observed, in each of the *fermented* grains of which the whisky was made but it is not quite lacking in any portion of the whole quantity of the whisky even when such a portion is quite separated and taken away from the whole in the cask. But is consciousness ever found, say, in an arm of the body, or in the solid or liquid matter which constitute the ingredients of the arm, whether before they had been built into or when they are detached from the body?*

*** Sânkh. Sû., iii 20 and 22 with Vijñâna and Ani. on them. I have interpreted the Sûtras slightly differently according to what I believe to be their original import.**
See also Cha. Kâ., Vol. II., p. 139.

Nor can it be maintained that, although consciousness may not be the property of the material ingredients of which the body is composed, it is produced by a combination of them *in a particular way.* That is to say, it belongs to, or inheres in, the particular *form* which they produce by their combination. For, consciousness as a property cannot inhere in anything but in some real entity; and a form cannot be said to be a real entity, inasmuch as it has no independent existence of its own.

Consciousnes cannot be due to the 'form' of the body.

Moreover, if it be held that there is consciousness in the various ingredients of the body, then it will follow that the consciousness of an individual really is the combination of an immense number of separate consciousnesses. But nobody feels himself as such, that is to say, as many. We all feel ourselves as one and the same individual.

Consciousness being a property of the body, individual consciousness would be only an aggregate of consciousnesses.

Not only does an individual not feel himself as many, but if really many consciousnesses formed one individual consciousness, then the body would often be either torn to pieces or absolutely inactive. For, it is comparatively a very rare thing to find a large number of conscious entities acting together absolutely with one will and purpose. They generally have different wills and purposes of their own, and if the different members and parts of the body had each a separate consciousness of its own, and at the same time were not subordinate to some other and central consciousness, it is pretty certain that they would often disagree and try to carry out their different wills and purposes; and the result would be a complete disintegration of the body. Or, if the body did not disintegrate, there would be an absolute deadlock of activity, inasmuch as the varying wills and purposes of the different parts of the body would neutralise one another. But as neither this kind of disintegration nor stagnation is ever observed, we must conclude that it is not the separate consciousnesses of the different parts of the body which produce the one individual consciousness.

Perhaps it may be said, that in the event of disagreement, the functions of the body would be carried on by the agreement of the majority. This may often happen. But it is also possible that sometimes the division may be equal and in such circumstances the body is sure to be divided into two parts. No such case, however, is ever known.

If consciousness were a property of the body then there could be no consciousness of the body as a whole.

Finally, it would be equally futile to urge that the will and purpose of the different members of the body, would be controlled and overruled by the will of the body *as a whole.* For, on the theory that the individual consciousness of a man is merely an aggregate of the consciousnesses of parts, there can be no meaning of the will of the body *as a whole,* except the aggregate of the wills of its different constituents. For, if it be held that the body as a whole can have its own consciousness and will, as distinguished from, and independent of, the aggregate of the consciousnesses of its various factors, then, such consciousness can be either essential or accidental. For, it cannot be anything else, as there is not a third alternative.

Consciousness cannot be essential to the body.

But if it were essential to the body, then there would be no death at all, for death is not possible unless consciousness is gone from the body; and it could not leave the body if it were an *essential* property of the latter. That which is an essential property of a thing cannot possibly leave it; as, for instance, impenetrability, which, as an essential property of matter, can never be absent from it. If it were essential to the body it would be, say, like colour which, being essential, is always with the body as long as it is. Colour is never absent from the body, because it is essential to the body; but this cannot be said of consciousness. It does not endure as long as the body does. Bodies can be found without consciousness, not only after death, but also in a trance or swoon. Therefore consciousness cannot be essential to the body.

Of course, here it may be urged that, although there is no absolute want of colour in the body, there is, at any rate, change of colour. A man, for instance, having white leprosy, will change his colour altogether. Yet, in spite of this change, colour cannot be said to be the property of anything but the body itself. Similarly, what we call consciousness and unconsciousness are merely two properties of the body, one alternating with the other, just as one colour can change into another. This argument would indeed be valid, if it could be proved, that unconsciousness were really a positive property, which could be contrasted with consciousness as one colour can be contrasted with another. But unconsciousness is not such a positive quality. It means only the absolute want of consciousness. That is to say, unconsciousness in a body, as at death, means not the production of a new property, similar in nature, as one colour is similar to another, but the absolute elimination of consciousness. There is no such absolute elimination of colour from the body as long as it lasts. It is true that one colour may succeed another. But there is always *some* colour in the body, as long as the latter is. This cannot be said of consciousness. It is, therefore, not the essential property of the body.

Consciousness accidental to the body.

But if it is not its essential property, then it must be admitted to be accidental to the body, for, as stated above, there can be no third alternative. And if it is accidental, it is evident that the body alone is not the cause or basis of consciousness. There must be something else, some other power or substance, which must come in, so to say, and in some way be related with the body before consciousness is produced in the latter.

And this can be done in two ways, as may be illustrated by two examples; namely, (*a*) the reduction, say, of solid gold or silver into a liquid or molten state; and (*b*) the lighting up of a room, say, with a candle or some other source of light. In the first example, that is, in the reduction of solid gold to a liquid state; the liquidity is the property of the gold *itself*, although it is produced by means of some other agency, which is introduced, so to say, from outside. In the second example, the illumination of the room cannot be said to be the property of the room itself, the light belonging to the *source* from which it proceeds. Now the question is: Is consciousness, produced in the body, of the nature of the liquidity produced in solid gold, *i.e.*, belonging to the body itself, although produced by means of some other agency; or, is it the property of the outside agency itself, as the light in the room is of the source of light, which is other than the room itself?

A little reflection will show that consciousness, produced in the body, cannot be the property of the body itself. For consciousness implies, as everyone knows, a relation, namely, between that which is conscious and that of which it is conscious. And it must be admitted that, whether they be essentially one or different—and we shall see that they are different—these two, things are quite distinct from one another at the time when the one is conscious of the other. And if this is admitted, it will further be conceded that of the two it is the first to which consciousness belongs, or, of which it is a property. Let us put the matter a little more concretely. Whether it be absolutely fixed and unchangeable, or ever varying, there is what may be called an "I-ness" in me, and when I am conscious of something, then whatever constitutes my "I-ness" at the moment is, and must be, distinct from this something of which I am conscious. Further, the consciousness at that moment belongs to *me*, that is to say, what constitutes my "I-ness" at the time. Therefore, it is the property of this "I-ness" in me, and not of that of which I am conscious. This fact, expressed in general terms, means that consciousness is not the property of that *of* which one is conscious, but of that which *is* conscious. In other words, it is not the property of the object of consciousness. But body is an object of consciousness; the latter, therefore, cannot be its property.

Being accidental to the body, consciousness need not necessarily be a property inherent in the body.

In any case, whether consciousness be produced in the body like liquidity in solid gold, or like light in a dark room, if it be admitted, as it must be, that consciousness is accidental to the body, and that, for its production in the body, there is, and must be, the need of some other agency, then the theory that consciousness is dependent entirely and exclusively upon the body falls to the ground. For, it has to be admitted that consciousness is produced by the combination of the body *and* something else. This being admitted, it is unreasonable to maintain, as the materialist does, that consciousness is the property of the body only, when it may be equally claimed to be the property of that some other agency, which must come into relation with the body before consciousness can be produced. As a matter of fact, for the reasons stated above, and for others to be mentioned now, it will be found more rational to hold that consciousness belongs to, and is the property of, this other agency rather than that of the body.

Consciousness and will must belong to the same Reality; but will cannot belong to the body.

That consciousness cannot be the property of the body will be seen from the following further considerations.

It must be admitted that a desire

or will is caused by consciousness. One cannot desire a thing or have any will to act with reference to a thing, unless one is conscious of the thing. Will, in other words, is a phase of consciousness itself. This being so, consciousness must belong to the same thing to which will belongs. Now, if it can be shown that the will does not belong to the body, it will follow that consciousness does not belong to it either. That will does not belong to the body, is clear from the fact that will is different from that which it moves. "The will of the carpenter moves his tools. The will of the warrior moves his sword. And the will of the boy moves his ball."* In other words, we all move material things by our wills and we know we are different from these material things. And if other material things are moved by wills which are different from them, it must be admitted that the will which moves the body itself, as it does move, must be different from the body, because the body is also a material thing. That is to say, it must belong to, and be the property of, something else than the body. Hence, as will and consciousness are inseparable, consciousness must also belong to that something else to which will belongs and not to the body.

Consciousness being property of the body would be perceived by other bodies.

Moreover, if consciousness were a property of the body, it would be perceived by others than the owner of the body. For properties of material things are perceived by all who are provided with the necessary senses. But the consciousness of A can never be

* Cha. Kâ., Vol. II., p. 152.

perceived by B. Therefore it cannot be the property of the body which is a material thing.

Consciousness belongs to what makes use of the body.

Again, we find that all made-up things are so made up by, and for the use of, others than the things themselves. A house is a made-up thing, and it is made up by and exists for the use of a man, that is to say, a something other than the house itself. This will be found true of all made-up things. And the body is a made-up thing. It must, therefore, belong to something else other than the body by which it is used. But it can be used only by a something that has consciousness; that is to say, the consciousness belongs not to the body but to that which uses it for its own purposes.

Consciousness belongs to what feels itself to be the possessor of the body.

Then again, there is the universal feeling of the body being a possession, and a possession implies a possessor. This possessor shows itself in a general way every time a man says: 'It is my body.' But it shows itself most strongly and clearly when a man has, let us say, a diseased arm or leg amputated, and he says or feels: 'I, as possessor of the body, have given up a part of it.' And if there is a possessor of the body, it is clear that consciousness belongs to that possessor and not to the body.

There would be no consciousness at all if it were a property of the body.

Moreover, if consciousness were the property of the body, there could be no consciousness at all. For the body, like any other material thing, is an object of consciousness. And if consciousness were a property of the body then that would mean that the property of a thing had the thing itself as its object, which would be tantamount to saying that a thing acted on itself. This is impossible. One might as well say that fire can burn itself. And as a thing cannot act on itself, that is to say, cannot have the thing itself as the object of its operation, and as consciousness of the body must have the body as its object of operation, there could be no consciousness whatever if it were a property of the body.

Inability to realise consciousness apart from the body does not necessarily prove it to be a property of the body.

Then again, our inability to realise consciousness apart from the body is hardly conclusive proof of the theory that experience is the property of the body.* We can indeed be certain of the existence of consciousness and all that it implies as long as the body exists in a living state, but we cannot be so certain of its complete non-existence when the body does not exist. For it is *equally* as possible that even after the body has died, the consciousness should continue to exist in some other state, as that it may altogether cease. And should consciousness persist, after the death of the body, it cannot surely be the property of the latter. In any case this very doubt is enough to prevent our accepting as truth the theory that consciousness is a property of the body.

Body may be a mere auxiliary.

Moreover, if it is concluded that consciousness is a property of the body because it takes place where there is a body and does not take place where there is none, we may as well conclude that visual perception is a property of light because it takes place where there is light and does not take place where light is absent. But as we can never accept this second conclusion as valid there is no reason why we should accept

* Shâr. Bhâṣh., III. iii. 54.

the first. For who can say that the body is not a mere auxiliary to consciousness as light is to visual perception?

Consciousness can be had without the body.

Finally, it is not true that the body is absolutely required as an auxiliary of consciousness, as we shall see later on.* While thus the chief argument in favour of the contention that consciousness is a property of the body is not conclusive, that theory cannot be accepted, for reasons given above, even as a possibility.

Consciousness cannot be merely a function of the brain.

And if consciousness cannot be a property of the body as a whole, neither can it be a mere function of the brain.† This brain theory of consciousness was never advanced in ancient India; but it has been treated by a modern Hindu philosopher of a genuinely Hindu school and education.‡ It has been shown by him that the brain theory of consciousness is open to exactly the same objections as the one which maintains that consciousness is a property of the body as a whole. Brain may be indeed needed as an instrument for the expression of consciousness, as the body as a whole is needed. But it is not a question of an *instrument* of consciousness that we are now considering. The point at issue is one of the *basis* in which consciousness *inheres* as a property. The argument that when the brain is in order there is consciousness, and when it is out of order consciousness vanishes, can only prove that brain is needed for the expression of consciousness; but not that consciousness is inherent in the brain or that it is a property of the same. It might as well be said that vision is inherent

---

* *Infra*, p. 149. † *See* Note 27. ‡ Cha. Kâ., Vol. II, pp. 174 *et seq.*

in the eye ; because if a man has his eye in good order he has good vision and if it is out of order he sees badly. All that such a fact can prove is that the eye is merely an instrument of vision, but not that vision is inherent in the eye. In the same way the brain may be merely an instrument of consciousness but there is no fact known which can prove that it is the basis in which consciousness is inherent as a property.

Âtman is that in which consciousness inheres.

Thus, as consciousness cannot be the property of the body or brain, it must belong to and inhere in something—some Reality which is other than and independent of the body. This Reality is called Âtman or the ultimate self of an experiencing being.

Without an Âtman there can be no memory.

That such an Âtman exists in each experiencing being will also be evident by a consideration of the problem of memory. If there were no Âtman independent of and other than the body, there could be no memory of the experiences we have had through our bodies. For the body of a man, like that of any other living entity, is at no time a *mere* aggregate of the parts and particles of which it is composed. It is, on the contrary, a secondary unit or an organic whole (Saṅghâta* or Avayavin) which is very different from, and something other than, a mere aggregate. If the body were a mere aggregate of particles, then the experiences which a man as an individual has through, and by means of, his body would be merely an aggregate of the experiences

* For this use of Saṅghâta *see*, among others, Vivaraṇopa., pp. 106 to 109.

which the different parts and particles have as separate, independent and independently conscious entities. But this is a position which we have seen cannot be sustained. No one can possibly conceive of himself, it may be repeated, as any but an individual and individually whole experiencer or conscious entity, and not a mere aggregate of a number of separate ones.

Body is an organic whole, i.e., a secondary unit.

This being so, we must regard the body as an organic whole, that is, a something which is, perhaps more, and certainly other, than a mere aggregate.

And if it is an organic whole, and if there be no other individual and no Âtman beyond the body, then the impressions and memory of experiences which a man has as an individual must be retained in the body as *a whole* and not specially in any parts or particles of it as separate entities.

But if it is true that the body is not a mere aggregate of particles but an organic whole, and that experiences are had, and impressions thereof retained, in only the body as such *a whole*, then, in the life of, and *as*, an individual, these impressions cannot possibly be transmitted from the body of infancy to those of youth and manhood and from the bodies of youth and manhood to that of old age.

Body as an organic whole is entirely different at different stages of life.

For these bodies *as wholes* are not one but entirely different from one another, and impressions inherent in one whole cannot possibly migrate into some other and separate whole.*

---

* *See* Note 28.

The point may perhaps be made clearer in the following way :—

Let a, b, c, d, e, f, etc., be particles of matter which come into, and compose, the body at different stages of life; and let the body in youth be composed of a, b, c, and d. Then, for reasons stated above, the body of youth will be not merely the aggregate of (a+b+c+d), but an *organic whole*, composed no doubt of these particles, but, as an *organic whole*, a different entity altogether and quite distinct from the mere aggregate of the components. Let this new entity be called α.

Now α, but *not* the mere aggregate (a+b+c+d), being the body of youth, the impressions of that age are, for reasons given above, inherent not in the mere aggregate of the components but in the new entity α.

Now suppose some of the particles pass out and others come in, some to take the places of the particles that are gone, others to add greater magnitude to the body; that is to say, let the body pass from youth to manhood. At this stage let its component factors be :—

$$e + f + c + d + g + h$$

namely, e and f as substitutes for the old particles a and b, and g and h as additional ones. Here again the body, *as an organic whole*, is not the mere aggregate of the components, nor even an entity representing

$$[(e+f)+\{\alpha-(a+b)\}+(g+h)]$$

but a totally new entity β. It cannot be simply

$$[(e+f)+\{\alpha-(a+b)\}+(g+h)]$$

for two reasons. First, this would mean that this new body of manhood is a mere aggregate of components which in this case would no doubt be the new particles coming in *as particles*, joined together with α as a whole *minus* some of its original factors. But we have seen that a body is not, and cannot be, a mere aggregate of components and therefore it cannot be merely

$$[(e+f)+\{\alpha-(a+b)\}+f+g].$$

Secondly, when β is produced there exists no α at all, so that *as* α it could enter into the composition of β. For α was an organic whole consisting of certain definite factors; and when some of those factors were removed, α *as* α ceased to exist; and what remained behind was not $\{\alpha-(a+b)\}$, but merely the particles c and d. These latter, together with the other and newly added particles produced a new organic whole, a new entity β, which must be totally different from α,—as different as x is from y, or a from b.

This being so, there is absolutely no connection between α and β. Therefore the impressions inherent in α cannot possibly pass on to β. And as they cannot pass from α to β and from β to γ, that is, from the body of one stage to that of another, there can be no memory of youth in manhood, or of manhood in old age. But such memory exists. We must, therefore, conclude that there must be some other entity above and beyond the body in which impressions of experiences inhere and which does not change with the changing body, but remains with them all, connecting α with β and β with γ. And because it remains with them all, it carries on the impressions of one age to another and thus makes memory of different ages possible. This entity is the Âtman.

It has been suggested that, as the body does not change at once, impressions could be retained as the shape and form is retained in fossils. This argument would be valid if the body were a mere aggregate; but we have seen it cannot be so. It not being a mere aggregate, the organic whole changes every moment, *as a whole*, but not bit by bit as the dead body of an animal or plant changes into a fossil.

Finally, it may perhaps be argued :—

Dogmatic assertions passed as reasoning. The strange position of one denying Âtman.

We know that particles change; we also know that impressions persist and memory is a fact. We must, therefore, suppose that impressions are *somehow* transferred from old particles to the new ones; but we need not suppose that they are retained in something else, which is other than the particles themselves.

We *might*, indeed, argue like this, *if* we could positively prove that there really *is* nothing beyond the body; and the argument in those circumstances would be quite valid. But nobody has so far positively proved that there is no Âtman. In the absence of any such proof, the above style of argument is only another name for merely dogmatic assertions. And it is the more objectionable, because the weight of evidence distinctly points to the existence of something beyond the body, of which consciousness is the property and in which impressions inhere. If, in spite of all the evidences in its support and of their reasonableness, we do not admit the existence of the Âtman, we are driven to invent explanations which are either merely dogmatic assertions, only thinly veiled as in the line of argument just referred to, or so absurd and chimerical that it is difficult to see how people can accept *them* and yet refuse the doctrine of the Âtman which, as a matter of fact, is the simplest.* If we admit that an independent Âtman exists, we explain things in the simplest way and we see at once how it is possible to remember experiences even when the body is completely changed.

Self-identity proves Âtman.

That there is, in each sentient being, an Âtman which is independent of the body, is also evident from the feeling of self-identity. For not only does a man remember the experiences of childhood in manhood, and of manhood in old age, but he feels himself really to be one and the same being at these different stages. He never thinks of himself as many in the same way as he does of his bodies. He feels and can say : 'I who saw in my childhood my parents, I, the same being, now in my old age, see my children and my grandchildren.'† This is the universal experience. From this, it must be concluded, that the entity which feels itself as thus being present and associated with all these ever-changing and mutually exclusive bodies, is different from them all. For, it may be laid down as a principle that, "if a thing remains the same in the midst of a number of changing or mutually exclusive things, then the thing existing with and accompanying them all, is different from the changing and mutually exclusive things. For instance, if, in the midst of a large number of flowers which are different from one another and mutually exclusive, we find a thread that runs through them all and makes a garland possible, then it is certain that the thread is different from the flowers."‡ Similarly,

* Cha. Kâ., Vol. II, p. † Bhâmatî, Intro. ‡ Bhâmatî, pp. 2 and 3.

although the body of childhood, youth and old age are mutually exclusive, there runs through them the thread of that something which perceives itself as the I, and therefore, this something must be different from, and other than, these different bodies. And because it is different from the different and changing bodies, and because it is with every one of them all the time, while they are changing, it is possible for man to remember the experiences of his childhood and youth in old age. If it were not so there could be no memory of childhood or youth in old age.

"Theory of Brain-selfhood."

As stated before, the theory that consciousness is only a function of the brain was never advanced in ancient India. The above arguments are directed against the theory that consciousness or experience is the property generally of the body, and that there is no Âtman above and beyond such a body. But they can be used equally against the modern European " theory of Brain-selfhood" as it has been called in Sanskrit (Mastiṣhkâtmavâda).*

'Psychical phenomena' as proofs of Âtman.

That there is an Âtman, independent of the body in each of us, would be still more evident, if we could take into consideration some of those facts, which are now being investigated by the 'Society for Psychical Research.' But these are facts which are not yet generally recognised as such in the West. The labours of the Society for Psychical Research may, in time, prove them to be facts for the scientific West. The Hindus think they know them to be facts, and bring

* Cha. Kâ., Vol. II, p. 175.

them forward as evidence of the existence of the independent Âtman. But in view of the general Western attitude in regard to these facts, I shall omit the arguments which are based on them.*

Without Âtman there can be no moral law.

Further, it could be shown that, if consciousness were the property of the body, and if beyond the body, there existed nothing else, that is, no Âtman, which is not produced or destroyed with the body, then there could be really no moral law in the Universe, and there could be no justice whatever.† If it be admitted that there *is* justice in the Universe, then it will also have to be admitted, as will be shown later on, that man's consciousness is not the property of his body, but that there is a something else in him which is different from the body and which has lasted from all eternity and will last for ever.

Body is not the Âtman.

But even without any reference to the moral bearing of the question at issue, perhaps enough has already been said to show that consciousness is not the property of the body, and that there is an Âtman which is independent of the body and in which consciousness inheres.

Âtman can neither be identified with senses, vitality or mind.

And if consciousness is not the property of the body, and, therefore, the body is not the Âtman, neither is consciousness the property of, and one with, those powers and faculties of man which are known as

(*a*) the powers of sensation, or sense-perception, that is, the senses;

---

* For instances of such arguments see Bhâmatî, Introduction, p. 3.

† Nyâ. Bhâsh., III. i. 4 (implied).

(b) vitality (Prâṇa); and

(c) what may be called the Mind (Manas).

And therefore none of them is Âtman, the sustainer of consciousness, in an experiencing entity.

Why Âtman cannot be the same as senses.

The Âtman in which consciousness inheres and which, therefore, is the real experiencer, cannot be any of the senses because a man sees a thing with his eyes, and feels it to be hot or cold with his temperature-sense and then he relates the two things together and says: 'It is one and the same thing that I have felt and seen.' This could not be possible if the experiencer or Âtman were not different, both from the eye and from the temperature-sense. The eye cannot feel the temperature of a thing, nor can the temperature-sense have visions. Nor can the eye say 'I who am seeing now have also felt the temperatures of something,' any more than the temperature-sense can feel: 'It is I who have both the feeling of temperature as well as vision.' Therefore it must be admitted that there is beyond, and different from, them both a something which relates the experiences that are received by means of both. This something is the Âtman which cannot, therefore, be the same as the senses.

Then again, we are aware of the senses as organs, that is, instruments by means of which things are experienced. But instruments, being used, always imply an agent which uses them, and without which they cannot be used. Therefore the senses being used as instruments there must be some agent which uses them.

This agent is the Âtman ; and, as agent, it cannot be the same as the instruments used.

Finally, senses are, as we have seen, things produced by Paramâṇus and Âkâsha and as such belong to matter ; and matter, as we have also seen, cannot have consciousness as its property.

How vitality is not the Âtman.

Nor can the Âtman be the same as vitality. For, vitality cannot possibly have any other meaning than merely the special relation of an Âtman with a certain form of matter which, by this relation, the Âtman organises and builds up, as a means of having experience.* And as long as this special relation lasts, all the processes of life, such as breathing and moving, handling and so on, are going on.

Mind and Âtman are different.

Finally, Âtman cannot be the same as the mind. If by mind we mean merely thoughts, ideas, and feelings, it is obvious Âtman cannot be any of these. For all these are continually changing, and they are known and experienced as such changing things in much the same way as the body and its changes are known and experienced. And being so experienced, they can no more be the Âtman than the body can.

But if by mind is meant a changeless something, by which all these thoughts and ideas are experienced, as much as the changing body and sensible objects are experienced, then, it is obvious, it must be different from the experiencer who experiences things by its *means*; that is to say, who uses it as an *instrument*. For, being

* Kandalî, p. 263, line 20.

used as an instrument of experience, it can no more be the same as the experiencer than the eye or the ear can.

Finally, if by mind is meant that something which knows and experiences thoughts and ideas, as much as it experiences the changes in the body, then, that would be merely another name for Âtman. For, as their experiencer, it will have to be distinguished, on the one hand, from the thoughts, ideas and feelings of which it is aware, and, on the other, from any instrument, by means of which it may be aware of them. And if the experiencer is so distinguished from both of these latter classes of things which are generally called mind, then it matters little by what name it is called. One may call it mind, if one likes. But in reality it will be the same thing as the Âtman. Thus it will be a difference of name only. The fact that the experiencer, whether it be called Âtman or Mind, will have to be distinguished from thoughts, ideas and feelings, which are commonly called mind in the West, and from any instruments by means of which these may be experienced by the experiencer cannot be denied. And if one prefers to call the former mind he will have to find a different name for the two latter classes of things. That is all.

Thus we find that there exists the Âtman which is independent of and different from the body, senses, vitality and mind, and as such constitutes the eighth Reality taught by the Realistic standard.

Âtman is eternal.

This Âtman exists in each conscious being, and is, and must be, eternal. For it cannot either be produced or destroyed. If it be held that it is a thing produced, then we must be told how it is produced, what it is that occasions its production, or what the material is out of which it is produced. If it be said that it is produced with the body, then that will involve all those objections which have been urged against the theory that consciousness is one with the body. And if it is not produced with the body, it cannot be shown to be produced in any other way either. And, if a thing is such that its origin cannot be shown, then it must be held that it also persists for ever. That is to say, as it cannot be shown that Âtman is produced from something else, it must be held that it is eternal.

Âtman is infinite, i.e., all-pervading, or in touch with everything.

Being eternal, it must also be infinite, that is to say, all-pervading or in touch with all things. For, it cannot be like a mathematical point without any magnitude. And a thing to be eternal, must either be a point without magnitude, or must be all-pervading.* Anything between these two, that is to say, anything of measurable magnitude, must consist of parts. And consisting of parts, it must be divisible; being divisible it cannot be eternal. Therefore, the Âtman, being eternal, cannot be conceived as of measurable magnitude.† Nor, as just said, can it be like a point without magnitude. If it were, the Âtman would not feel itself, as most people do, one with the whole body which is extended. Therefore the Âtman is infinite, that is, all-pervading.

We shall see later on, that the whole universe is moulded into shape by the acts of Âtmans. This would be impossible, if they were not in touch with all

* Kandalî, p. 92, lines 20 and 21. † Sid Cha., leaf 12 (1st side).

things. We shall also see that while the different parts of the Universe constitute spheres of experience for the different Âtmans, there must at least be one Âtman which has the Universe as a whole for its sphere of experience.* This means, that this Âtman is in intimate relation with, and has control over, all things.† This is possible only because that Âtman is all-pervading, *i.e.*, in touch with all things. And if one Âtman is all-pervading, all other Âtmans must also be the same. For, there is no reason to suppose that *in essence* they are in any way different from one another. The only difference which there can be between the different Âtmans is, that while they are all in general touch with all things, they have intimate and special relations which are different, *i.e.*, more or less extensive, in different cases.

An infinite number of Atmans.

Then again, there is an infinite number of Âtmans, as many as there are or can be living and conscious entities.‡ If there were not, everybody would be conscious of the feelings and thoughts of everybody else.

Âtman only sustains consciousness and experience.

Finally, the Âtman in each is undoubtedly the Reality in which all consciousness inheres. But consciousness or experience is not its *essential* characteristic.§ These are produced, and inhere, in it, in the same way as sound is produced, and inheres, in Âkâsha. How they are produced will be seen when we come to deal with what I have called the Synthetic aspect.

---

* Kandalî, p. 88, lines 11 *et seq.*

† *Infra*, p. 123, *et seq.*

‡ *See* Note 29.

§ *See* Note 29.

The Manas.

The existence of the next and final class of Realities, namely, Manas, is supported in the following way.*

Evidence of Manas.

We have seen that the Âtman is the basis of consciousness and experience. It is in that, that consciousness inheres. But the Âtman is all-pervading, and therefore it is always present everywhere, always in contact with every sense. The senses again come into special relations with sense-objects, which are then perceived by the Âtman. But it is observed that the Âtman does not always perceive an external object, even when the latter is in relation with a sense, or senses, by which it is perceived. The Âtman is *there*, because it is present everywhere, and always; and the object may also be there, and its relation to the sense, by means of which it is perceived, may be there too; and still the perception does not take place. This happens not only when one is deeply absorbed in one thing to the exclusion of others, but under ordinary conditions. What is the reason of this? The only way in which it can be explained is this:—For the perception of things the Âtman requires not only the senses, but something else as well, which being absent, the object in question cannot be perceived, even when it is in relation with the senses by means of which the Âtman can perceive it. When this something, the missing link, is supplied between, so to say, the Âtman and the senses, and thereby a *special* relation is established between the Âtman and the object, then at once perception takes place. It must be there, otherwise there is no reason

* For full reference on this section, *see* Note 30.

why there should not be any knowledge and any perception, even when the senses are in relation with the sense-objects. This something is called Manas.

Succession in experience proves Manas.

That the Manas exists, is also seen from the fact that we can know things in succession. The Âtman being present always and everywhere, there is no reason why things should be known in succession. This succession of knowledge can be explained by the fact that knowledge is got by the movement of Manas, which now connects with this thing, and now with that; and this enables the Âtman to know things one after the other.

Manas is needed as an organ for experiencing thoughts, feelings and so on.

Then again it is observed that the Âtman, which is the only experiencer, is conscious of the sensible objects, such as colour, odour, and so on, by means of the sense-organs. We never know a sense-object without the use of an organ. But these are not the only objects of which the Âtman is conscious. It is conscious of such things as pleasure and pain, that is to say, of the objects of the nature of feeling. And, if in the case of every one of the sense-objects, the Âtman has to use an organ, an instrument, by means of which alone, it can perceive its object, it is only reasonable to infer that, in the case of the objects of other classes also, of which the Âtman is conscious, it has to use an organ.

Recollection of things forgotten also proves Manas.

Then there are those objects of consciousness which the Âtman knows as thoughts and ideas, and which are sometimes present as actual objects of consciousness, and sometimes disappear, to be remembered again when the occasion or need arises. Both for the knowledge, for the first time, of these thoughts and ideas, as well as for calling them back to memory, when they are for the time being forgotten, or at any rate, are not prominently before the Âtman as conscious objects, an organ is needed.

Organ is needed for experiencing thoughts and feelings.

Nor can it be said, that while the organs are certainly needed for the perception of the sense-objects, no such instrument is required for the awareness of pleasure, pain, thoughts, ideas, and so on, because they are purely subjective or internal. For, the fact that thoughts and ideas are sometimes known, and sometimes forgotten, shows that there must be an instrument which makes such a phenomenon possible. It cannot be said that the ideas that are now forgotten, but can be remembered with some effort, are absolutely absent from the Âtman. They are somewhere in the Âtman. How is it then that they are not always remembered? The only explanation is that there must be some organ, without the use of which the Âtman cannot be aware of things, which are retained even in itself; and that in order to be aware of, *i.e.*, to remember, any one of them, the Âtman has to direct this organ towards that thing or object, when it rises up, so to say, in consciousness again; that is to say, is remembered. And this something which may be directed by the Âtman to this or that object of thought or idea, which may have been forgotten, but is remembered now, is Manas.

Only one Manas in each.

This Manas, in each sentient being, is only one, not many, as indicated by the fact that we can be conscious of things in succession. If there were more than one

Manas in a man, there would be simultaneous perception of many objects even when succession was desired. For, there is no reason why, when a man fixed one Manas to one thing, the other Manases should not be bringing about perception in regard to other things.

It might perhaps be said here that although there may not be more than one Manas, as there are more senses than one, for the perception of *variety* of objects, yet there may be a plurality of mental organs. For, if the perception of sense-objects requires the sense-organs *as well as* the Manas, the awareness of mental objects should require the Manas *plus* something else. This would undoubtedly be the case, if the mental objects were, even when in relation with the Manas, sometimes known and sometimes unknown, as the sense-objects are even when they are in relation with the senses. But that is not the case. There is, therefore, no need to suppose that there may be some other organ behind the Manas. There is, therefore, only one Manas in each, not many.

Manas is eternal.

Manas is also eternal. For it cannot be conceived as being produced, as there are no simpler factors or parts out of which it could be produced. And if it is not produced, it must be indestructible and therefore eternal.

Manas has no magnitude whatever.

Being eternal, it is without any magnitude. For, as said before, an eternal Reality must either be of infinite magnitude, like the Âtman, or without any magnitude.* All others, being of limited or measurable magnitude, are divisible into component parts or factors, and

* Kandalî p. 92, lines 20 and 21.

therefore perishable. But as eternal Manas cannot be of infinite magnitude, it must be without any magnitude whatever. It cannot be of infinite magnitude, because if it were, there could not be any succession of perception or forgetfulness and calling back to memory. For, Manas has no special and specific qualities of its own, such as odour, flavour, luminosity, temperature, or sound or consciousness: therefore it cannot be considered as having any special relation with anything. Being without special qualities, and therefore without special relations, if Manas were also of infinite magnitude like Kâla and Dik, it would be equally and generally related with everything at the same time; and, as a consequence, there would be an equal and simultaneous knowledge of everything on the part of the Âtman. In fact, in that case, there would be no necessity for a Manas. Âtman by itself would experience all things all at once. But Manas is wanted to enable the Âtman to have experience, not simultaneously of all things at once but in succession. We must, therefore, regard Manas as not of infinite magnitude. And not being of infinite magnitude and yet being eternal, it must be without any magnitude whatever.

Manas moves extremely quickly.

Being without magnitude, it must be conceived as a thing which is capable of extremely quick movement. For, otherwise, there could not be those perceptions of things which seem simultaneous.

Manas and Âtman.

Such a Manas, it is obvious, is quite different from the Âtman which must be conceived as of infinite magnitude and as the basis of experience, whereas the Manas is only an instrument of experience.

Finally, there must be an infinite number of Manases, as there are an infinite number of Âtmans, one in each experiencing entity.

An infinite number of Manases.

The Principles Summarised.

These, then, are the Realities which are found to constitute the world, when the same is examined from the Creationist or Realistic standpoint. There is nothing else which can be called absolutely real, that is to say, self-subsisting; and all the infinite variety of things in the Universe, all facts of experience, can be explained by these factors, and their attributes. And the recognition of these factors of the Universe may be called, as suggested before, the *analytic* aspect of the Universe from the Creationist standpoint.

Before we pass on to an exposition of what may be called the synthetic aspect of the Universe from the same standpoint, and see how all phenomena can be explained by means of these factors, let us first, for the sake of convenience, recapitulate the principles.

These are :—

(1-4) Four classes of Paramâṇus, which are without any magnitude, but are self-subsisting and *super-sensible* Realities. They are the forces, stimuli or things, which produce the perceptible objects having temperature, colour, flavour and odour, as their special qualities, besides others which constitute their general qualities;

(5) The Âkâsha, Ether or Ethereal Space, which is an all-pervading Reality of infinite magnitude. It provides the expanse, room or space in which all discrete things

move and serves as the medium of connection between discrete and separated things. It is also the background in which sound as an intangible and ethereal quality inheres;

(6) Kâla, or the principle or force of universal movement, which urges things onward; and by bringing them into existence, changing and finally carrying them out of existence, gives rise to the notions, in the percipient, of past, present and future, of old and new;

(7) Dik, or the principle or force which holds things together in their various relative positions even while they are being driven on by Kâla; and thus gives rise, in the percipient, to the notions of 'here and there,' or 'near and far;'

(8) The Âtmans, which are the bases of consciousness and experience in all experiencing entities and are eternal and infinite. Being of infinite magnitude, they are, every one of them, in general touch with everything, but they come into special relation with one or other object as its experiencer by means of the Manas and senses; and

(9) The Manases, of which there is only one in each experiencing entity. This Manas in each is the force or power, which is the direct instrument of knowledge and experience. Manas is without any magnitude whatever and therefore non-spatial.

Of these, the four classes of Paramâṇus and Manases are without any magnitude whatever and are discrete and infinite in number, and Âkâsha, Kâla and Dik are each a single reality having universal scope and operation; while the Âtmans are Realities which have each equally universal scope, but are infinite in number.

B—THE SYNTHETIC ASPECT.

So far I have dealt with what I have called the analytic aspect of the Universe from the Creationist or Realist standpoint. In order to give a complete general outline of it, I shall now present the main doctrines which constitute the Synthetic aspect as taught in this Realistic system. But, as stated before, the Synthetic aspect, in its broad outlines, is exactly the same in all the three standards and is not peculiar to the first. Being common, the main Synthetic doctrines of the Realistic system have been treated by writers on the Sâṅkhya and the Vedânta. Moreover they follow almost as inevitable conclusions from what has been said before. I shall, therefore, just mention them now, giving an occasional argument here and there when it may seem necessary.

The doctrines constituting the Synthetic aspect may be stated as follows :—

No first beginning of things.

1. There is no creation of a universe,—that is to say, an orderly arrangement of things into a system,—which is absolutely the first creation. The beginning of a universe means the beginning of a system only, which under no circumstances is the first and only one created. On the contrary, it is merely one of a beginningless series.* Thus if the present universe, as we find it to-day, had a beginning,

* Vaish. Sû., V. i. 13. (implied) Nyâ. Bhâṣh., I. i. 19, III. i. 27 ; (towards end) ; Ât. Tat. Viv. ; Prashasta, pp. 48 and 49 with Ki. Va. and Kandalî on the same ; Saptap. Mit., p. 8, line 14 ; Vivṛ., IX. ii, 7 ; Shâr. Bhâṣh., II. i, 34-36 ; *see* Note 31.

there was another before it and if that one came into existence at some point of time, there had been another which had preceded it, and so on. This beginningless series of universes is called Saṁsâra* (lit. the constant moving on; or being born and dying repeatedly.)

That Saṁsâra is beginningless can be supported as follows :—

Meaning of a first beginning of Saṁsâra.

An absolutely first beginning of the universal process can mean only one or other of the following alternatives :—

(i) That it was a first moulding or fashioning, of their own accord, as a Universe, of the ingredients which were already existent, and had been existing for ever without a beginning.

(ii) That such eternally existing ingredients were moulded into the Universe by an intelligent being (or, which is the same thing, beings).

(iii) That it was created by an intelligent being out of nothing.

In the first alternative, the stuff must have existed for ever; in the second, not only the stuff, but the being, who moulded it into the Universe, must have existed for ever; and in the third alternative, it is the being that must have existed from all eternity.

In any case it must be admitted that something had existed from eternity and prior to the creation of the Universe.

Age of the Universe and Eternity.

Now the age of the Universe, however long, is yet limited, and must have begun, on the theory of a first creation, at a definite

---

* On the meaning of Saṁsâra, *see* Note 32.

point of time in the past, however remote. And this age, however long, is surely insignificantly small as compared with the beginningless, that is, the eternal duration of the stuff or of the being, that is, God, as such a being would be called.

In view of this fact, it will be seen that on none of the three alternatives can a first beginning of the Universe be maintained.

The first, meaning of an absolute beginning, is impossible. No self-movement of inert matter.

On the first theory, namely, the stuff fashioning itself of its own accord into the Universe, we have to ask if this stuff is something intelligent, that is, can start movements by itself, or if it is of the nature of inert matter. In the first case, it will not be very different from the being of the second theory, which we shall deal with directly. In the second case, how can an inert something start a new movement by itself? No inert matter can possibly start movements of its own accord, and as nothing can be shown to have come, so to say, from outside, to operate on the inert stuff and thus produce movement, it must be concluded that there have been always movements in this stuff, and therefore there has always been a creation, a moulding of the Universe.*

No beginning of Samsâra if activity be essential to God.

On the second and third theories, namely, of a being, that is, God, having moulded the Universe out of eternally existing stuff, or of creating the Universe out of nothing, we have to ask: Is this moulding or creative activity essential to God or merely accidental?

* Shâr. Bhâṣh., II. ii. 2. (implied). *See* Note 33.

If essential, then it has existed eternally with God; for nothing that is essential to a thing can be conceived as being ever absent from it.* And if the moulding or creative activity has always been with God, then a Universe also has always existed as a result of this activity. Nor will it do to say, that while activity is no doubt essential to God, it had existed from all eternity as a potentiality; and that only at a certain point in the remote past, it began showing itself as an actual process. For, even then it will have to be explained how a something which had existed from all eternity as a potentiality, could suddenly manifest itself as an actuality. And as this cannot very well be explained, we must maintain that the creative or moulding activity, if it is at all essential to God, has always existed as an actuality and not as a potentiality.

Creation impossible if activity be accidental to God.

If, however, it be held that the activity is not essential to God, but only accidental, then He must have come by it at the time when He began moulding or creating the Universe. But how, whence, and in what way did He come by it?† There is hardly any *reasonable* way of showing how a being that had remained perfectly satisfied without activity from all eternity, could suddenly start creating a Universe.

A first beginning is morally indefensible.

Even if we grant that God, not being unintelligent matter, could make such a sudden resolve, our difficulties are not solved. For, unless we dogmatically assume that in the beginning all were created alike, we cannot

* Shâr. Bhâṣh., II. i. 33. with Rat. Pr. *See* Note 34. † *See* Note 35.

maintain, without contradiction, that God, who is conceived as a moral and just being, could possibly ever have created a world so full of partiality and suffering.*

Nor is the contradiction removed by saying that God created all beings equal and endowed them with free-will; and that they by their free choice made themselves happy or miserable, good or bad.† For then the question will be: Why did He give free-will to created beings and thus make them behave one way or another so as to bring suffering and wickedness into the world? God is regarded as omniscient and He must therefore have known the disastrous consequences which His gift of free-will was going to produce in the world.

As a matter of fact, however, God cannot possibly be conceived as having created these suffering or enjoying beings, or, as they would be called, souls, if they are regarded as everlasting. For nothing that is created or produced can possibly last for ever.‡ There is no known example of it. Nor can the souls themselves be brought forward as examples of such produced but everlasting things. For that is just what will be disputed and will have to be proved; and a thing which has to be proved cannot be brought forward as an instance of ascertained truth.§ Moreover, we have seen that the real experiencers, that is to say, the Âtmans, must be eternal, uncreate and immortal.

But even granting, for the sake of argument, that they are created by God and endowed with free-will,

---

* Shâr. Bhâṣh. II. i. 34 and 35. † Rat. Pr., II. i. 34 (end; implied).

‡ A common Hindu notion; Comp., Nâstyakṛitaḥ Kṛitena, Muṇḍ. Up., I. ii. 12. § Cha. Kâ., Vol. I, p. 148.

our difficulties are not removed. For even then we cannot hold God to be just, impartial and free from cruelty, if not positively merciful, if we maintain that He created or moulded this Universe for the first time, and made it, without any reason, full of suffering and partiality.

No contradictions in a beginningless Samsâra.

All such objections and contradictions are removed entirely, as we shall see, if we accept the view that the universal manifestation never began, but that it is and has for ever been; and that, in short, it is an eternal process which has gone on for ever and ever.

This beginningless process of universal manifestation, or series of Universes, is called, as said before, Saṁsâra.

The Universe consists of various grades of existences. The sensible and super-sensible worlds and beings.

2. The next doctrine is that the Saṁsâra consists of various orders of experiencing beings, inhabiting what may be called various worlds or modes of specific existence.*

In regard to the worlds, the existence of the sensible is obvious to all.

But we have seen that the originating sources of the sensible are themselves super-sensible realities. And in addition to these there are the Âtmans with their various Saṁskâras and Adṛiṣhṭas—things to be explained presently. There are also the Manases which serve as the direct instruments of experience on the part of the Âtmans.† There is no reason why these in themselves as

* Vaish. Sû., IV. ii. 5-11; Nyâ. Bhâṣh., IV. i. 55; N. V. T. Ṭ., p. 441, line 14 (over.)

† Prashasta, pp. 49 and 280; Shâr. Bhâṣh., IV. iii; Sâṅkh. Sû., III. 46-52 with Vijñ. and Ani. Sâṅkh. Kâ., 44. and 53, with comms. *See* Note 36.

super-sensible Realities should not constitute another order of things, besides the sensible—other worlds or spheres, which we may call the transcendental or super-sensible. Not only is there no reason why they should not constitute such super-sensible worlds, but there is every reason to believe that these worlds, constituted by the transcendental entities *as transcendental*, exist. For, as we shall see, a world or sphere of existence is nothing but a condition of the experience on the part of experiencing beings; and therefore there must be as many varieties of worlds as there are fundamentally different types of beings.

In regard to these beings, we find that there are, in the sensible world, a great variety of them, and that they form themselves into a number of orders and grades. These grades, we also find, form a series, one extremity of which lies in that order of beings, whose experiences are the most limited.* Beginning from this grade, as we come up towards man, we find what may be called an ascending series, each successive order in which is found having experiences which are wider in range than those of the beings of the preceding order.

In this way finally we come to man, who undoubtedly stands at the head of this series. But there is no reason to suppose that man is absolutely the highest order. On the contrary, seeing that man is limited and that he is often frustrated or unexpectedly helped in his endeavours by unseen powers, we must admit there are beings who are higher and more powerful than men, and who exist in unseen forms.† If what is super-sensible

*** Shâr. Bhâṣh., I. iii. 30, p. 180 M.**

† Based on Bṛih. Up., I. iv. 10, with Shânkara Bhâṣhya on it.

in man can exist in an unseen form after death, why not other beings who habitually exist in such forms?

And if these beings exist in unseen, *i.e.*, super-sensible forms, then there are also states of existence or worlds which are also super-sensible.

In this way we find that there are in the Saṁsâra different orders of things, *i.e.*, different worlds sensible and super-sensible, as there are different orders of experiencing beings. Man belongs to one of them.

Man—how he is constituted.

3. And a consideration of the nature of man leads us to the next doctrine of the Vaisheṣhika. It is, as already implied in the analytic part, that man consists of*:—

(i) A body and senses, which are produced out of the four classes of Paramâṇus and conditioned Âkâsha.

(ii) Manas, by the operation of which the awareness of the different things and memory are, on the part of the Âtmans, made possible. It is eternal, but without any magnitude whatever.

(iii) The Âtman which is eternal and infinite.

Âtman in man is the experiencer.

Of these three, it is the Âtman which is the real experiencer and the Âtman gains its experience of the world by means of the body, not immediately, but through the intermediate link of the Manas; without the Manas it can have no experience whatever, as without it there can be no awareness of things.

Âtman as agent.

And, as the real experiencer, the Âtman must also be the agent of activities which are at least voluntarily performed.

---

* *See* Note 37.

Two-fold results of Âtman's activities.

As a result of these experiences and activities the Âtman has produced in it:—

(i) Certain tendencies, faculties or character (Saṁskâra).*

(ii) Certain potentialities of relation or moral worth (Adṛiṣhṭa).*

Saṁskâras—how produced.

And the way in which Saṁskâras, *i.e.*, faculties and character, are produced can be perhaps best illustrated by an example like the following.

Let us suppose a boy studies mathematics, say, Euclid, to be more definite, and becomes very proficient in it. Then, later on in life, he takes up, let us suppose, some profession or trade where he has absolutely no use for Euclid as such, and as a consequence forgets, say, in 20 or 30 years' time, all that he learnt as a youth of Euclidean Geometry. He may even forget the very first definition. But he can never shake off the mathematical bent which his mind has received. This will follow him at every step, and guide and determine his mode of thinking. This bent, tendency or capacity, is what a Hindu would call a Saṁskâra—a mathematical Saṁskâra in this case, produced by his study of mathematics, of which the details may be entirely forgotten.

Saṁskâra is general memory.

But what is this Saṁskâra in reality? It is obvious it can be nothing else but a *general impression*, that is to say, a *general memory* of activities or experience as

* *See* Note 38.

distinguished from their details, which, as in our illustration, may be entirely forgotten. But while the detailed memory, or memory of the details of experience may disappear, the Saṁskâra as *general memory* is not gone.

And, as in the case of the mathematical, so in that of all other Saṁskâras or tendencies and capacities, they are produced by experiences and activities of other sorts and are the general memory of them as distinguished from their details, which may be equally forgotten.*

So far then with regard to Saṁskâras as one of the results of activities. But before we leave this question we must take into consideration a few more incidental things.

Details of experiences may be entirely forgotten but not lost.

We have seen that when the Saṁskâras are produced, the details may be forgotten. We are forgetting details of experience every day. It often requires a great effort of memory to recall minute details of experience which a man had only yesterday. Thus while we are forgetting details always, this forgetfulness in some cases may be so complete that hardly a trace is left. That this is so in regard to details of experiences had as infants is obvious. As an illustration of such complete forgetfulness of the experiences of adult life take the remarkable Hanna case, as given by Drs. Sidis and Goodhart in their "Multiple Personality." In this case every trace of memory of his twenty-four years' existence was entirely lost by Mr. Hanna after an accident

---

* *See* Note 38.

and he had to start life again as a new-born baby does, but with *tendencies and aptitudes* which were those of Mr. Hanna, as he was previous to the accident. And it was with the greatest difficulty that memory of the past existence previous to the accident was brought back, and the two Hannas—as the two separate groups of experiences may be called—were united into one whole.*

But that the memory of the past could be brought back shows that, though entirely forgotten, it was not absolutely lost.

Although there are not perhaps many cases recorded by European psychologists of such complete forgetfulness of the whole of the past, and its eventual recovery, examples are not wanting of complete forgetfulness of *part* of the past experiences, and their calling up to memory. Several such cases are known to students of hypnotism.

While these are examples from the West, there are many in the East. All these show that :—

(i) The Saṁskâras are produced by experience and activity; and incidentally,

(ii) They are only general memory of the experiences;

(iii) The details of these experiences may be entirely forgotten, like the details of experiences had in infancy;

(iv) But because they are forgotten they are not lost;

(v) They can be brought back to memory;

(vi) Forgetfulness of the past experience, even when complete, does not prove its non-existence in the past; and finally,

---

* *Multiple Pers.*, pp. 83—326.

(vii) They are retained in the experiencing Âtman, as they must be, for reasons given in the analytic part.

So far then with regard to those results of experiences which are called Saṁskâras.

As for potential worth or desert (Adṛiṣhṭa), that is, the second class of results produced by experience, let us see how that too comes about.

Adṛiṣhṭas—how produced.

When a man is born he finds himself in a body of a particular kind, and in a certain situation and environment. What birth can really mean and why he finds himself in that particular body and that particular situation, but not in another, will be considered later. That he is born in a particular situation is obvious. Now, it is observed that, being born in a particular body in a particular situation, a man can, within limits, make his body and situation either better or worse. That is to say, he can make them more or less conducive to his happiness by acting one way or another. For instance, he drinks, and thereby brings on disease, and thus makes his body a source of misery for himself; or, he observes strictly the laws of health and keeps the body in good condition so as to derive nothing but happiness from it. Or, in regard to his situation, he behaves in such a way that he makes all his relations, and those who surround him, most unfriendly to him; or, he renders services to them and makes them all helpful and grateful to him. While thus he can change his body and situation one way or another, if he chooses to do so, by behaving differently, the behaviour which would improve them and make them more conducive to his happiness and therefore better for him, together with the thoughts, ideas and feelings which will lead to such behaviour, may be called the right behaviour or conduct for him in that particular body and situation, and one which he should follow in that body and situation; while that conduct of his and those thoughts and feelings leading to it which would make his body and environment *worse* for him, may similarly be called the wrong conduct, which he should refrain from pursuing. In this way it can be ascertained which is the right conduct for a man in a particular body and situation, and which is wrong; and definite rules can be laid down so as to be able to say that such and such conduct, being right, would be conducive to his true happiness, while other conduct being wrong would produce suffering for him.*

While this is possible, and while there are cases where we may know absolutely which the right or wrong conduct is, we yet find that a man following it does not change his body or situation one way or another immediately. He may sometimes meet with results of his conduct immediately, but often he has to wait for them. Thus, for instance, a man may go on indulging in all kinds of excesses and yet may long escape the consequences. Again, although doing nothing but acts of kindness, a man may yet find himself surrounded by people who continue to be ungrateful to him, and make his life miserable, until, when he has waited for some time, he finds a change in the situation. Again, a man who is constantly cheating others, may yet for long find

---

* For the Nyâ.-Vaish. idea of the 'Moral standard' see Ap. A, p. 177.

these very victims of his, his friends, until one day he is caught and sent to prison. Why the results of conduct for some time are thus postponed will appear later on, but that they do have to wait for manifestation is a fact. It is happening every day in our life, not only in one direction, but in all,—the results of conduct, right or wrong, waiting for fulfilment. But when the results appear, they alter a man's relation with his body and situation. They may, therefore, be called the *potential relations* of the man to certain bodily conditions and situations, as distinguished from his actual relation to the body and situation which he possesses at the moment. This actual relation again may be said to represent what may be called his cash-value or worth, as, for instance, when we say : a man has such a fine or miserable body, such good or bad circumstances, so many friends or enemies, so much wealth or so much poverty, and so on. And if the actual relation to a body and situation is his worth in cash, the potential relations of a man may be called his worth in possibilities or, simply, his potential worth. And it is this potential worth which is called Adṛishṭa in Sanskrit and constitutes the second group of results of experience.*

Thus a man is constantly producing by his experiences :—

(i) Saṁskâras, or tendencies, faculties, or simply character, on the one hand ; and

(ii) Adṛishṭa, or potential worth, on the other.

---

*On the use of the word 'Potential' in this connection, and in Nyâya-Vaish. generally, *see* Note 39.

These results are had, as said above, really by the Âtman. For it is the Âtman that acts and has experiences and thereby produces Saṁskâras and Adṛishṭa.

But of course the Âtman acquires them, just as it has the experiences, when in relation with a body. But as any particular body is produced and has a beginning, it is obvious, that the relation with it, of the eternal Âtman, (by means of the Manas), also begins.*

Meaning of birth, death and life.

When this relation of the Âtman, by means of the Manas, with a body begins, the Âtman may be said to be incarnate. And while it is really the body, which is born, that is to say, is produced in a particular way, yet the Âtman may also be said to be born in a figurative sense, meaning thereby the beginning of its relation with that body. Similarly, the death of the body may, in a figurative sense, be spoken of as the death of the Âtman, meaning simply its dissociation from that body. The Âtman being eternal can have no real birth and death, if by these terms are meant the production and destruction of a thing of which they are predicated. The Âtman can only come into relation with and be dissociated from a body.

While thus the birth and death of a body, with which an Âtman comes into relation, may be figuratively spoken of as the birth and death of the Âtman itself, the period during which the body lasts may be called an incarnation of the Âtman, and the latter spoken of as living during this period.

---

* Vaish. Sû., Upask., V. ii. 17 ; Vivṛ., VI. ii. 15 ; Nyâ. Vâr., III. i. 19.

Using the words birth, death and life in the above senses:—

Âtman in man is born again and again. Doctrine of Re-incarnation clearly stated and all that it implies explained.

4 (i) The eternal Âtman of a man, together with the eternal Manas, which is its primary and immediate instrument of gaining experience, is born and dies not once but countless times. It has gone on doing this for ever and ever, *without a beginning*, in an equally beginningless series of universes.*

(ii) As it does so, each successive birth or incarnation and its possibilities are determined absolutely and in every respect by the Adṛiṣhṭa and Saṁskâra acquired in the previous incarnation or incarnations—Adṛiṣhṭa and Saṁskâra, without which the Âtman has never been, because its series of incarnations never began.† "It reaps exactly according as it has sown."

The Adṛiṣhṭa and Saṁskâra determine:—

(*a*) The locality and time, environment, circumstances, possible associations and so on of and in the new birth.

(*b*) The family and parentage, with which, on the one hand, the Âtman is linked by Adṛiṣhṭa; and which, on the other, can offer it at least some affinity of Saṁskâra, *i.e.*, of character and tendencies both of body and

---

* Vaish. Sû., Upask., Vivṛ., V. ii. 17; VI. ii. 15; Prashasta, pp. 280 to 281, 308 and 309.

† Nyâ. Sû., Nyâ. Bhâṣh., I. i. 19; Nyâ. Vâr., IV. i. 10; III. i. 19, 22, 25, 26, and 27. *See* Note 40.

mind, so that the latter in the re-incarnating Âtman can find some scope, however small, of manifestation, and thereby can get its deserts in the direction of what may be called his subjective being, as distinguished from his objective situation, possessions and circumstances—that is to say, all that is meant by 'heredity.'

(c) The *possible* period during which that incarnation can last, *i.e.*, possible longevity.*

(iii) The Saṁskâras also show themselves as the innate tendencies, capacities and possibilities of character in which children differ from one another.

(iv) But the Adṛiṣhṭa and Saṁskâra determining a fresh incarnation, or Saṁskâra showing as innate character and capacities of the child, need not necessarily be, and, as is obvious, often cannot be, exactly those acquired in the immediately preceding life.

Postponed Adṛiṣhṭa how possible.

Owing to our varied kinds of activities we are daily acquiring worths and tendencies which are often so incompatible with one another that they cannot possibly be actualised together.† Thus, for instance, a man may acquire two sets of worths; one of which, when actualised, will make him, let us say, poor and miserable from birth, while another will give him a most comfortable and luxurious situation, also from birth.‡ It is obvious these two sets of worths cannot actualise themselves together.

* Vivṛ., VI. ii. 15. † Nyâ. Bhâṣh., IV. i. 64.

‡ Prashasta, p. 281; Kandalî p. 53, line 13; Upask., VI. ii. 16; *see* Note 41.

When one set is operating the other must wait till it finds an opportunity ; just as seeds sown in the ground, and then covered with snow, must wait till the snow melts away before they can germinate. This is also the reason, why, in our daily life, many of our acts do not bring about their consequences at once. In fact, it is by virtue of this principle that any potential worths are at all produced. Otherwise, all activities bringing about their results at once, all worths would be only cash-values.

And what is true of Adṛishṭa, is also true of Saṁskâras. We cannot simultaneously be both sentimental and cool and calculating; or, at the same time both sickly and robust.

Thus Adṛishṭas and Saṁskâras often being incompatible with one another, some will have to wait (and wait even for long), when others are operating. And it is out of this waiting Adṛishṭas and Saṁskâras (which may be of many lives of the past, and even of a very remote past), that a certain portion may determine the next birth of a man ; while the Adṛishṭa and Saṁskâra which are being acquired now, may have to wait long for their turn. That is how it may happen that the next incarnation of a man may be very different from what one could possibly expect from his present conduct and character. A bright and keenly intellectual man may be re-born, as a sentimental fellow, and a saintly man may re-appear with many an evil tendency in his nature. Or, one, who has tried all his life to help others, may yet find himself in very undesirable and unfriendly surroundings.

But, of course, none of the Saṁskâras or Adṛishṭas of a man are lost.* They wait, as it were, behind him, and form a sort of reserve in the background. It is perhaps this reserve which, it would seem, is now being recognised in the West as the 'sub-liminal self' of a man.

Nothing is lost. 'Sub-liminal self.'

However that may be, the point to note is, that not all the tendencies and capacities which we are now forming or showing in our lives, nor all the worths which we are now acquiring, may show themselves in our next incarnation. Some of them *may* re-appear in the next birth, or they may all sink down, for a time, into some deep strata of our being, while others may crop up.

In every case, however, any capacities and tendencies, which may show themselves as inborn in a child, or any circumstances in which it may be born, are only things *acquired* in the past and are not 'gifts' as they are often called.†

No 'gifts.'

The above ideas together constitute what are called the doctrines of Re-incarnation and Karma (lit., activity, meaning moral causation due to activities which in their turn produce Adṛishṭas and Saṁskâras).‡ But in reality they form only one doctrine, which in the Nyâya is called simply 'Pretyabhâva.' We shall refer to the two doctrines together as 'Re-incarnation,' except when Karma will have to be specially mentioned.

Re-incarnation.

---

* *Ibid.*

† Kandalî, p. 53, line 1. *See* Note 42.

‡ *Supra.*

Arguments in support of Re-incarnation. As for arguments in support of Re-incarnation the Nyâya simply says:—

That the Âtman re-incarnates is established by the very fact that it is eternal.*

This statement of the ancient Nyâya, in so far as it relates to the existence of the Âtman previous to its birth in a body, finds a strange parallel in a most modern writer, I mean Dr. Mc Taggart, who says:—

"Any evidence which will prove immortality will also prove pre-existence."†

The Hindus, however, are of opinion, that, if pre-existence of Âtmans is admitted, then, from that very admission, will follow, as an inevitable consequence, the doctrine of Re-incarnation also. Hence they have been satisfied chiefly with refuting the idea that the Âtman is a perishable thing. And this notion being recognised as refuted, by every body in India, the truth of Re-incarnation was never questioned.

That is perhaps how Re-incarnation has been so commonly accepted in India. And it being a universally accepted idea among Hindus of all shades, as well as by Buddhists and others, although they have differed as to the exact mode of its operation, none of these people have troubled themselves very much to establish its truth, *as a fact*, by argument. Still there are many arguments which can be adduced in its support. Of these the following is one‡:—

We have seen that an Âtman, during life, is always acquiring Adṛiṣhṭa or Potential Worth. And Adṛiṣhṭa always means possible relation to a new situation.

* Nyâ. Sû., IV. i. 10. † *Dog. Rel.*, p. 113. ‡ *See* Note 48.

But much of this Adṛishṭa must relate to situations of the same kind in which it is acquired inasmuch as much of the activities, by which Adṛishṭa is acquired, affect things and beings existing in that same kind of situation or state. That is to say, some of the Adṛishṭa acquired in a human state must relate to a human state, which may, *still as a human state,* be higher or lower than the one in which Adṛishṭa was acquired. Similarly, some of the Adṛishṭa acquired by a superhuman being existing in the super-sensible world must relate to a superhuman state, and so on. We may call this kind of Adṛishṭa, the Adṛishṭa of the same or similar state, or simply *similar* Adṛishṭa, as distinguished from Adṛishṭa which may produce relations with a situation or state of a *kind other* than the one in which it is acquired.

Now there is no man who, at any moment of his life, is without some Adṛishṭa of the same state. For, by our actions, we are always affecting others existing with us in the same state, and always having the consequences of *some* of these acts at any rate postponed. This being so, when a man dies, the Âtman must still have in it some Adṛishṭa of the same state. This means that the Âtman has potential relations with a situation of the same kind in which it acquired the Adṛishṭa. If the man does not die at the time when we are supposing him dying, and, if he contiuues to live till the Adṛishṭa of the same state, which he would otherwise carry with him at death, becomes an actual relation to an actual situation, then, it is obvious, that the situation that would be produced as the result of that Adṛishṭa would be one of a similar kind in which it was acquired, that is to say, a *human* situation on this earth. And if on his continuing to live, the Adṛishṭa would actualise itself into a situation on this earth, there is no reason to suppose that, simply because he dies, that situation when actualised would change completely and be something other than human and earthly. And if an Adṛishṭa of the same state, acquired during earthly life, can produce a situation, to which the Âtman is bound, only on this earth, then it is certain, that the Âtman, dying with any Adṛishṭa of the same state, must be re-born in the state in which the Adṛishṭa was acquired. And as most men have some Adṛishṭa of the same state when they die, it is obvious they must all be re-born on earth.

Further arguments in support of Re-incarnation.

That the Âtman is born again and again will be evident also from a consideration of the folloing points *:—

The body of a man has a beginning as surely as it has an end; but the Âtman, as we have seen, is eternal; and being eternal, we cannot think that it has been lying naked, so to say, from all eternity, without an embodiment of some sort. If it could lie naked all these countless æons, why should it suddenly come to be born? It cannot be said that an Âtman suddenly makes a resolve to be born and is born. For, in that case, we have first to show the antecedents which can lead to such a resolve; because we know of no resolves which are made without antecedents consisting of thoughts, ideas and perceptions. Secondly, if an Âtman

* *See* Note 44.

came to be born out of its own choice, by making a sudden resolve, it would be born only under conditions which could make it happy. But there are millions of men that are anything but happy in regard to their situations or bodies; and it is unlikely that the Âtmans in them would have come to be born out of anything like choice.

Nor can it be said that it is born, once and all of a sudden, entirely by chance. For, there is a rigid law which guides and governs the body in which the Âtman is born, (that is to say, with which it is related) and the surroundings in which the body is found. This body and surroundings form one term of the relation, while the Âtman forms the other. In these circumstances it is hardly reasonable to assume that, of the two terms of a relation, while one is guided by law, the other is merely a thing of chance.

Finally, if it be held that it is God who associates the Âtman with a body, and He does so only once, then such a God would be open to the charge of injustice and involved in contradictions.* He would be unjust and malicious, inasmuch as He associates one Âtman, without any reason, with a body where a man cannot but be happy and have pleasant surroundings, while He associates another with a body which can be only a source of misery, and surroundings which can only foster vice. But nobody thinks of God as being unjust or whimsical, and therefore the theory that God associates an Âtman with a body, only once, without any reason, must be abandoned.

* Brah. Sû., II. 34-36, &c.

And if God cannot associate the Âtman with the body only once and for no reason, much less can He create the Âtman. For, in the first place, we have seen that the Âtman is uncreate and eternal; and secondly, even if it were created, God would be involved in just the same inconsistencies, and would be open to the same charge of injustice and whimsical conduct as in the case of his associating an eternal Âtman with a body once and for no reason; for we have to ask: why does he create and place some souls (as Âtmans in those circumstances would be called), in pleasant, and others in unpleasant or vice-breeding surroundings?

Re-incarnation and heredity.

Nor is it of any avail to say that all this can be explained by what is called heredity.* For the question, raised here, is *not*: *how* offsprings resemble their ancestors and parents in bodily characteristics or tendencies, or *how* they inherit circumstances from them. For that is hardly a problem; it is a fact which anyone can see. But it is: *why* we come to be born of particular parents, inheriting particular bodies and surroundings, and not of other parents of a superior or inferior nature, and inheriting different bodies and situations of a different character? In other words, the question is: *why* is a particular Âtman connected with one body rather than another? And finally, how it comes to have a body at all? It is a fact, let us say, that a man inherits a miserable body or surroundings, because his parents have miserable bodies and surroundings; and the question is: why does this man or Âtman come to be born in a family or

* *See* Note 45.

surroundings where everything is miserable, everything is conducive only to vice, and not where he can have everything in perfection?

Of course, if the existence of independent Realities like an Âtman be denied, as the Materialist may deny, then such a problem does not arise. But we have seen that, in order to account for consciousness, the existence of Âtman as an independent Reality must be admitted. And, if this is admitted, then mere heredity will not and cannot explain the problem. For, to repeat, it will then be: *why* does one of these Âtmans come to inherit a particular body and surroundings rather than another?

How inadequate the idea of heredity as an explanation of this problem is, can be perhaps best illustrated by the following example. Suppose a man renders service to a State, and thereby deserves a reward in the shape of some money. He gets this money, let us assume, from one of the State Treasuries or Banks with which the State has business. There may be several banks or treasuries of this kind all over the country; and the State, in view, say, of the nearness of his residence, or out of some other consideration, gives the man an order to receive the money from a bank in a certain part of the country. He goes to this bank, cashes his order and gets the amount. Afterwards, as he comes out of the bank with his cash, a crowd of people sees him do so. Then, suppose, these people as an explanation of our man's getting suddenly wealthy, say: he got wealthy because he got the money from the bank. It is obvious, this can never be the real explanation. That will have to be sought in the fact that the man deserved the wealth by his service.

In the same way, the explanation of the fact that we get different kinds of bodies and surroundings is not that we get them, or, which is the same thing, inherit them from our parents, but that we *deserve* to inherit them. And this deserving of ours again can be but the result of our past thoughts and deeds, retained as potential worths or Adṛishṭas in the Âtmans. Of course, we can get what we deserve, such as a good body or a bad body and so on, only in families where these can be had, as the money in our illustration can be had only from a bank or a treasury but not from a beggar's hut.

Thus the difficulties which beset the theory of a first and one and only birth of a man on earth are at once removed by the doctrine of Re-incarnation; namely, that the Âtman is ceaselessly repeating its births in a beginningless series of lives in a beginningless series of Universes (Saṁsâras); and that, of these births of the Âtman, the successive ones are determined, entirely and absolutely, in regard to their nature, heredity and environment, and even possible longevity, by the activities of the Âtman in the preceding ones, the Âtman suffering or enjoying exactly as it has acted in the past: it reaps exactly as it has sown.

Re-incarnation: memory of the past.

While Re-incarnation thus solves a number of difficulties, the only objection which can be seriously raised against it, namely, that we do not remember our past existences, will be seen to be based on erroneous notions. To begin with, it is not true that we forget entirely everything of our past experience; for a man does possess a memory of the past, a general memory, as we have called it, in the shape of tendencies, faculties and character; that is to say, as Saṁskâras. What is termed conscience in the West may also be interpreted as only a vague memory of the experiences of the past. Secondly, it is only the details of experience that are not remembered. But if the details of experiences can be forgotten by an accident, as they were in the case of Mr. Hanna, surely they must be forgotten when the old body in which the experiences were had goes to pieces, and a new body is formed. Moreover, we all forget the details of experiences which we had as infants and yet we do not doubt our infancy. But, as a matter of fact, even the details, as stated before, are not entirely lost. As we shall see, by suitable means, they can be, and the Hindus say, have often been, recovered.*

The question of memory, therefore, is hardly a real objection against Re-incarnation.

Before leaving this question of memory, it may be noted here in passing that one of the features which characterise a man of high type, such as a Ṛishi or a Buddha, is, according to the Hindus, this very fact that he does remember all his past lives and every experience in them.

Re-birth as sub-human and super-human beings.

By virtue of this principle of Re-incarnation the Âtman may be reborn (for every birth is only a re-birth) not only, as a man but, according to Adṛishṭa, in any of the lower forms of beings which are below man; or it may

* Upask., V. ii. 18; VI. ii. 16. Yoga Sû., II. 39, with Bhâsh. and Vṛit.

re-appear, by other Adṛishṭas, as one of the higher order of beings in the super-sensible world which, as we have seen, exists.*

How this is possible.

This is possible by so behaving during life, as to acquire Adṛishṭas not of the same state, but other Adṛishṭas productive of a dissimilar state (which we may call simply dissimilar Adṛishṭa); and by deserving thereby a situation of a sub-human or a super-human order.† An Âtman can acquire dissimilar Adṛishṭas by its conduct, because being all-pervading, it is at every moment of its life, in relation not only with the world of human beings but with various others. Being in relation with these worlds it can affect them by its conduct, (by its deeds, thoughts, and feelings) as much as it can affect the human world. And just as in consequence of affecting the human world in one way or another, it deserves in the same world a situation of this or that sort, so does it deserve different situations in the other worlds, in consequence of its affecting them in various ways.

All experiencing beings are Âtmans born in various states according to Adṛishṭa.

In this way it happens, that Âtmans that were born as human beings often appear, according to their Adṛishṭa, in all the varying grades of existence. In fact, the various experiencing beings, forming the different grades of the universe, sensible and super-sensible, are nothing but Âtmans born in these grades.‡ It is Âtmans alone which are the real experiencers, as we have seen. And the Âtmans are constantly

---

* Prashasta, pp. 280-281. † *Ibid.* *See* Note 43.

‡ Prashasta, p. 39 (bottom). *See* Note 46.

changing their situations for others of a similar or dissimilar character, according as, in any given situation, they behave one way or another, that is to say, according as they acquire Adṛiṣhṭa of one kind or another.

Hierarchy of beings—created by Adṛiṣhṭa or worth.

5. But as Adṛiṣhṭa always means relation, a higher or lower Adṛiṣhṭa, leading to a higher or lower situation, is nothing but a relation of a higher or lower order. This again can only mean a relation either of controlling or of being controlled.

And as birth in any grade or order is merely the result of Adṛiṣhṭa of one kind or another, to be born in a higher or lower grade, really means either to have control over, or be controlled by, others; just as in human life to be placed in a higher or lower position means to have power over, or be controlled by, others.

And so it happens that, owing to the working of Adṛiṣhṭa, all the experiencing beings, in a system or Universe, are brought into direct or indirect relation with one another and are arranged in a hierarchical order in which the higher orders control the lower.* In this hierarchy of beings, it is obvious, the highest is that which has control over all; and it can get to that position, as is also obvious, as a result of its own Adṛiṣhṭa, while the other beings occupy their respective places according to theirs.

Hierarchy produces system and unity.

This gives unity to the multiplicity and infinite variety of beings, and of the things under their control—and all things are under the control of, and serve as means

---

* *See* Note 47.

of experience for, some being or beings. And as it gives unity to the multiplicity, it makes of the latter a single system and an organic whole.

The Universe is created and exists for a moral purpose.

6. But if in this system and hierarchy, to be born in a particular situation, and to have a particular measure of control and influence over others, means merely the actualisation—more or less partial—of one's potential worth (Adṛishṭa), it follows that the various situations and spheres of influences are themselves nothing but the direct results of the worths themselves. That is to say, they are created by the Âtmans themselves by their own activities (Karma). That a situation, which follows immediately a certain act or acts done by a man, is created by that act or acts, nobody doubts. But, if an immediate consequence can be the creation of a particular act or acts, there is no reason why we should not regard deferred consequences of acts also as such. And as actualisation of Adṛishṭas is nothing but the realisation of the deferred results of acts performed in the past, all situations and spheres of influence in which beings are born or continue to exist by virtue of actualised Adṛishṭas, are as much the creations of their own acts of body or mind as those which follow immediately other acts which they may perform. And as every situation or grade of existence and sphere of influence in the Universe is only the actualisation of the Adṛishṭa of some experiencing entity, it follows that the whole Universe is a creation, or is a result of the acts of experiencing beings.*

---

* Prashasta, p. 48, line 19 (bhoga-bhûtaye); Upask., VII. i. 1; Sânkh. Sû., VI. 41; Ani., III. 51; Shâr. Bhâṣh., II. i. 34, &c., &c.

That is to say, the Universe exists for a moral purpose, supplying for the experiencing beings, their various situations and spheres of influence, according to their worths,—each situation or sphere of influence serving as a means on the part of a being getting its share of experience, its meed of joy or of sorrow and suffering according as it deserves. But if the Universe is merely an actualisation of the potential worths of beings and is created by the acts, and for the experience, of Âtmans, it is so created, (that is to say, moulded into shape) of course, out of the ingredients, and with the assistance of the various powers or forces, which have existed eternally.

A beginningless and endless series of Universes, all linked together causally. How the essences of the Universe alternate between phases of Chaos and Cosmos.

7. Then again, if the Universe, as it exists to-day, has been created as the result of moral worth on the part of the Âtmans, it must also come to an end some day. For the Universe as a whole exists for the experience of the highest being, (that is Brahmâ, *not* Brahman, as such a being occupying this position is called in Sanskrit), and as such it is merely the actualisation of his worth.* But worth, being acquired, must come to an end some day, for nothing that is acquired as the *direct* result of activities can possibly be unlimited. The worth of Brahmâ, therefore, must also come to an end; and when it ends, the Universe, which exists merely as the actualisation of this worth, will also come to an end.

But if the present Universe ends, there will arise another Universe in its place and out of the ruins of this

---

* *See* Note 48.

one. For beings are acquiring worth in this Universe as well and some one of them stands, in the universal hierarchy, next to the present Brahmâ. And when the present Universe perishes, much of this worth is bound to remain still unactualised, just as, in the case of an individual man, much of his worth remains still potential when he dies. And the potential and unrealised worth of the present Universe as a whole, as well as of the being standing next to the present Brahmâ, or, of the present Brahmâ himself, if his new worth would still permit him to occupy that position, must be actualised some day when the proper time and opportunity occurs. And when it is actualised, another Universe will follow.

But if this Universe will be succeeded by another as a result of the worths acquired in it, it must be concluded that the present Universe itself came into existence only as a successor of a past one, in which the present Brahmâ, and other beings, had acquired their respective worths.*

Similarly, the predecessor of the present Universe must have been preceded by another ; and so on without a beginning.

Nor need we think that this series of Universes will ever come to an end. For there is no reason to suppose that the number of Âṭmans is finite. And if they are not finite, that is to say, if they are infinite in number, then the flow of the Universes will go on for ever, even though some of them may and even actually do, as we shall see, cease to have Adṛishṭas and therewith the necessity of having experience and existence in specific forms.

* Ât. Tat. Viv.

Thus the series of Universes must be infinite, beginningless and endless.

In this infinite series, the successive Universes being the inevitable results of worths acquired in preceding ones, it also follows, that the series is held together by an inexorable law of cause and sequence.

Following this sure and certain law of cause and effect, a Universe or orderly arrangement of things, *i.e.*, a cosmos, comes into existence, out of what may be called chaotic and formless ingredients, and is again dissolved into the same chaotic and formless state, only to be succeeded by a new cosmic form. Or, as it may be stated: the ingredients are eternally alternating between the phases of a Chaos and a Cosmos. And if for ingredients we substitute Energy, and for chaotic and formless state, a potential phase, and for Cosmos a phase of explication, then this ancient Hindu teaching finds a strange corroboration in the words of Huxley, who says :—

"The faith which is born of knowledge finds its object in an eternal order, bringing forth ceaseless change, through endless time, in endless space; the manifestations of cosmic energy alternating between phases of potentiality and phases of explication. It may be that, as Kant suggests, every cosmic magma predestined to evolve into a new world, has been the no less predestined end of a vanished predecessor."*

In this process of alternation on the part of the universal Energy or ingredients, a complete period of explication, together with that of the following potential

* *Evolution and Ethics*, pp. 8 and 9.

phase, is technically called a 'Kalpa' (lit. Imagining or thinking), and its two phases Srishṭi and Pralaya, *i.e.*, Creation and Dissolution, respectively.*

And these periods succeed one another by virtue of Kâla, as seasons follow one after the other; as men are born, die and are born again; as they wake up and sleep; and as heavenly bodies whirl around in orbits, and occupy the same postions in the all-pervading Âkâsha again and again and in ceaseless succession.†

Finally it is Dik which, when things are created, holds them in their relative positions as Kâla urges them on.

In this way the Universe goes on and on, and for ever and ever, its essence alternating eternally between 'phases of explication' and 'phases of potentiality.'

Justice in the Universe.

8. And as this alternation goes on, the beings, *i.e.*, eternal Âtmans in successive Universes reap exactly as they have sown in the preceding ones. Thus there is absolute justice in the Universe and nothing is undeserved.‡ This cannot possibly be said of the Universe if a God is thought to have created it for the first and only time.

'Nothing new under the sun.' All types of beings present always and therefore all types of ideas. Meaning of progress.

9 (i) Further, as the Âtmans are eternal, and all ideas and impressions are retained in them and are even remembered, in their entirety by Rishis and in part or as general memories or Saṁskâras by others, and as it is these Âtmans with past experiences which really build up

* Comp. Yathâpûrvam *akalpayat.* *See* Note 49. † Shâr. Bhâṣh., I. iii. 30; Ma. Bhâr., I. 1. 38-40. ‡ Kandalî, p. 53.

a new Universe,—it follows that a new creation proceeds along the lines of the old.* It is very much like the building up, by men of an old country, of a new colony wherein things are done naturally on the lines of the old. That is to say, there is behind a new Universe always the ideas, impressions, and experiences of various grades, high, middling and low, of a past Universe. This being so, it follows:—The past and old always reproduce themselves in the present and new. There is, therefore, nothing which is really and absolutely new. All appearances are but *re*appearances and 'there is nothing new under the sun.'

(ii) There is no time in the life of the Universe when any phase of thought and experience is wanting, although Âtmans having *all* types of thought and experience may not always be found incarnated on earth, or even in the sensible Universe as a whole.

(iii) Therefore, there is no such thing in the Universe as an absolute progress of all things, *all* starting at the same time from the lowest stage and then gradually advancing to higher and higher ones. Progress and evolution from a lower stage to a higher one is always with reference to individuals or groups of individuals, but never of the entirety of beings all starting at the *same time* from the lowest level.

---

* *See* Note 50.

Progress and evolution never a blind and unaided groping.

10. This being so, even the progress and evolution of any particular individual or group of individuals, from a low stage, is never a really blind and absolutely unaided groping.* For there being always in the Universe, though not necessarily in the sensible world, higher types of beings side by side with the lower ones, and the higher ones being, as they must be owing to Adṛiṣhṭa, in touch and relation with the lower, the former cannot but help and guide or at least influence the lower, with their own ideas and thoughts. These may be communicated physically if the higher beings exist in the sensible world. Otherwise such thoughts and ideas can be communicated to us "as inspiration," and as "sudden flashes," such mode of communication being possible on account of the fact that Âtmans in experiencing beings are always in touch with one another, whether incarnate in physical bodies or discarnate.

History of progress and philosophy of history.

The History of progress, therefore, must always be like that of progress in education made by a child.† The child does indeed progress and evolve from a lower stage to a higher one. But if, in writing the history of progress made by the child, one recorded only the different stages in the growth of the child, it would be only half the truth. The history, to be really true and complete, must take into account the fact that the child has had teachers, who have helped him and put before him ideas which they indeed knew by experience though their pupil did not.

---

* *See* Note 51.　　† *See* Note 52.

As this is how things generally progress and as the history of progress means merely the history of assimilation, on the part of the lower, of the already existing thoughts, ideas and achievements of the higher beings, the history of any science or philosophy, which embodies knowledge of true facts and principles and not mere speculations, must also take into account the fact that such knowledge had already existed before in higher beings, and was merely learned and assimilated by lower ones from them—the knowledge being received either through sensible means or as 'inspirations' and 'sudden flashes' or as super-sensible experiences of a very precise and exact kind, such as ecstatic hearings, visions, and so on.

No real beginning of knowledge. The Veda—how it is eternal.

11. Thus it happens that there is no real beginning of any Science or Philosophy which has in it any true knowledge of facts and laws in regard to the nature of things or of principles of conduct. That is to say, real knowledge (not mere speculation) of things and principles has no beginning at all. This beginningless knowledge (*a*) of the nature of things as they really are, and (*b*) of principles of proper conduct, has always been had by some being or beings in this beginningless series of Universes.*

And it is this two-fold knowledge or wisdom, direct and immediate, vast as the Universe and without a beginning, which is the Veda.†

It has always been directly known and realised by some beings in its entirety and by others in part.

* Cha. Kâ., Vol. V, p. 124 *et seq.*

† For the Vaish. idea of the Eternity of the Veda, *see* Note 53.

These beings are Brahmâ and the Ṛiṣhis, human and superhuman, of various grades. Of the Ṛiṣhis again those alone are perfect who have the Wisdom in perfection. And they, as a class, as well as inferior beings, as other classes, have existed eternally. And as the class of Perfect Ṛiṣhis have existed eternally, some of them have taught men that aspect of the Veda which consists of the principles and rules of conduct, following which men may rise from a lower to a higher state of existence, human and superhuman.*

Varṇâshrama Dharma.

This communicated knowledge of the rules and principles of conduct which, as is obvious, must be different in different cases according to the various natures and circumstances of the persons taught, is called Varṇâshrama Dharma or simply Dharma.†

This Dharma men may follow or not, either from choice or from imperfect understanding. If they follow it, they rise gradually in the scale of beings. If they do not practise the Dharma and do what can but lower their worth (Adṛiṣhṭa), they go down.

Constant rise and fall in states. How compulsory existence in specific forms is suffering.

12. And as all beings of imperfect knowledge and wisdom are liable to make mistakes in regard to the practice of Dharma, and as some of them violate Dharma through weakness, it happens there is always a climbing up and down of beings in the hierarchy of the universe.‡

---

* Nyâ. Bhâṣh., IV. i. 62 ; Prashasta, p. 258 (top), with Kandalî ; Upask., IX. ii. 6.

† Prashasta, p. 272 ; *see* Note 54. ‡ Kandalî. p. 281. *See* Note 55.

And even those rising constantly cannot have their superior places secured for ever. For the latter are gained only by worth. And as worth can never be unlimited and must come to an end, sooner or later, with the vanishing of worth, the position which is gained as a result of it must also be lost. In any case, to maintain a superior position in the hierarchy, one must always be on the watch lest his Dharma not being done properly he may be outdistanced by others. Therefore he can never have real and abiding Peace and Bliss.

Thus existence in any one of these rungs of the universal ladder is wanting always in permanent Peace and Bilss and is, in this sense at least, if in no other, full of misery, sorrow and sufferring.

Only way out of this suffering is to be freed from the necessity to be born in a specific form of existence.

13. There is only one way out of this ceaseless anxiety and constant possibility of falling down and suffering, if not actual sorrow and torment. And that way is to free oneself from the *necessity* of having any form of existence in any of the grades of the universal hierarchy at all—that is to say, to be absolutely free and really independent*—to attain Mokṣha or Mukti, as it is technically called.

This freedom gained only by realisation of truth, *i.e.*, true nature of things by direct experience.

14. And this freedom or Mokṣha can be had only if the Âtman is freed from activity (karma) of the kind which leads to worth and thereby to some specific form of existence—as existence as a member in the universal hierarchy may be called.†

* Vaish. Sû., V. ii. 18, with Upask. (opening line).
† Vaish Sû., I. i. 4 ; Nyâ. Sû. I. i. 2 ; Prashasta., 281 ; Nyâ. Bhâṣh., VI. ii. i. (Introduction), &c., &c.

But how is a man going to free himself from activity? Not surely by being idle. For that would mean simply not doing the duties of his position and will lead him in the end, not to freedom but to a specific existence of a very undesirable sort and perhaps to a stone like state. He may not, without disastrous consequences, shirk the duties of a position, once he has found himself in it. For, no living creature can live and yet be absolutely idle, and man can be no exception to this rule.* And if a man, while living, cannot be absolutely idle, that is to say, if he must be doing something, and yet if he does not do his duties, he cannot but produce some Adṛishṭas by those activities of his which he would be performing as a matter of necessity. These Adṛishṭas are bound to be of a lower nature and therefore drag him down. Such activities are bound to produce a lower Adṛishṭa because they will be done only with a view to self-gratification of some sort or other without any redeeming feature in them. He must, therefore, do what really are his duties in the situation; and, at the same time, he must seek Wisdom, that is, true and direct knowledge of the nature of things as they really are: that is to say, he must realise that aspect of the Veda which consists of such Wisdom.† For it is only by knowing, that is, realising by direct experience, the truth of things as they really are, that he can make himself absolutely free from activity that will produce Adṛishṭa and therefore existence in a specific form.

That nothing but realisation of truth can make one free in this way will be evident from the following

* Bhag. Gîtâ, iii. 5. † *See* Note 56.

considerations. It is activity with a motive to improve our body and situation, *i.e.*, to gain advantage to oneself or even one's race or country, as *opposed* to other individuals, races or countries, and their interests, that leads to worth and specific existence.* But such activity is possible only so long as men feel and think of things as their own special possessions, and not as belonging generally to all, and think of their special interests as opposed to the interests of others. And this mode of thinking and feeling again is due only to ignorance—ignorance of the true nature of things.

For one thing, it is ignorance of the true nature of things and beings in so far as the perceptible forms of these are cencerned. These things and beings, as compounded and organic wholes, look so pretty and beautiful or so hideous and repulsive.† Appearing thus, they give rise in our nature to likes and dislikes; to desires to possess them, or to aversion. And these in their turn lead to activities with a view to gain some advantage.

But if we really know, *i.e.*, realise by direct experience (and not merely as an intellectual conviction produced by reasoning), the true nature of these, they no longer have such powers over us. For then we realise them to be but shapeless and formless Paramâṇus, all alike, and therefore incapable of distinction as hideous or attractive.

Then again, it is the ignorance in regard to the true nature of the Âtman. This ignorance, for one thing,

---

* Prashasta, pp. 280-281. † Nyâ. Sû., Nyâ. Bhâsh., Nyâ. Vâr., IV. ii. 1-3 ; Nyâ. Bhâṣh., IV. ii. 1 (introduction).

makes a being regard, of the particular body or form with which the Âtman happens to be related, as itself or himself. With this feeling it clings to it, longs to perpetuate it. And when it breaks up and the Âtman is reborn in some other form, it clings to that form again and thus it goes on for ever and ever. And as it clings to these forms or embodiments, and thinks of one of them at a time as itself, it is led to activities with a view to securing advantages to that particular embodiment in opposition to the interests and advantages of other beings in other embodiments.

But if the true nature of the Âtman is realised, and a man can feel by direct experience that he himself is the Âtman, then there can be no clinging to any form and no fear that the form being destroyed, the Âtman will perish. A man who has realised himself as not the embodiments but the Âtman, can never work with a view to any advantage whatsoever to himself in opposition to others. Such advantages or disadvantages belong, it is obvious, only to the specific forms of existence which are different from one another but not to the Âtmans as such. For the Âtmans are all alike. Nor can he work with a view to gaining advantage for one particular race or people as opposed to other peoples and races. For no race is his, or rather all races are his. He is the Âtman and as such does not belong to any race. It is the body that belongs to a particular race. Thus realising the true nature of the Âtman, all motive for working with a view to gaining for himself any advantage in any form, as opposed to the interests and advantages of others, that is, other individuals and races, altogether ceases. And the motive ceasing, such activities cease; and activities of this character being absent, no potential worth is produced; and when there is no potential worth there can be no birth into any specific form of existence.

Thus with the ceasing of ignorance, both with regard to the essential character of things and in regard to the Âtman, and with the realisation of their true nature, all causes of births in specific forms are removed and the Âtman is really free.

Wisdom therefore, that is to say, the realisation by direct experience of the true nature of things, is the only means of getting out of all specific forms of existence and of realising true freedom.

15. But a man seeks this wisdom only when he is really tired of specific forms of existence—the feeling of this tiredness being realised not so much as a clear fact of experience in his surface consciousness but as a deeply rooted Saṁskâra.

Qualification of the candidate for the knowledge or wisdom. Teachers of wisdom. Its transmission.

Such a man, thus tired of being compelled to be born in specific forms of life, is also truly fit for Wisdom. And such fit candidates for Wisdom, like other types of beings, have existed always in the Universe. For, as we have seen, no types of being can ever be really wanting in the Universe. And if they have existed for ever, they have never had to grope after Wisdom in the dark.* If they groped long enough they might have hit upon it. But this has never been necessary. For if candidates for Wisdom

* Kandalî, p. 282, &c., &c.

have existed always, there have also always been perfected Ṛiṣhis, who have already realised this Wisdom by direct experience. These Ṛiṣhis have taught the worthy candidates who in their turn have learned and realised the truths and then, themselves becoming Ṛiṣhis and teachers, have taught others. And thus, like the Eternal Veda itself, the line of teachers and pupils has continued till this day.

The method of teaching and acquiring Wisdom. Three steps.

16. And the pupils have always learned and realised the truths by following a definite method. This method consists of three distinct steps, namely:—

(i) Receiving the truths as 'statements,' or propositions enunciating the truths; technically called 'Hearing' (Shravaṇa);

(ii) Understanding of the truths, thus received, by reasoning, *i.e.*, by weighing arguments both against and for—teachnically called 'Consideration,' or 'rational demonstration' (Manana); and

(iii) 'Realisation' of the truths by direct experience.*

First Step. The Propositions—how enunciated.

Taking the first step, the 'Hearing' can be accomplished, that is to say, the truths as statements can be received, as is obvious, only from teachers who have already realised them as they are. What, therefore, they say to enunciate the truths are the words of the

---

* Nyâ. Sû., Nyâ. Bhâṣh., Nyâ. Vâr., IV ii 47; Prashasta, pp. 281 and 282; Kandalî, p. 282; Upask., Vivṛ. IV. ii. 16; Saptap. and Mit., p. 32, &c., &c.

Veda. Hearing is, therefore, done 'in the Words of the Veda.'*

These truths which, following this first step, are thus 'heard' have been mentioned before; namely,—

The five Bhûtas are;
Kâla and Dik exist;
Âtmans are;
They are born again and again;

and so on.

This first step of the Hindu method of acquiring philosophic truths may not be improperly compared to the first step, *i.e.*, enunciation of a proposition, of Euclid in the matter of acquiring a geometrical truth.

Second step Rational Demonstration—how done. Philosophy is only rational demonstration of truths.

When the truths are 'heard in the words of the Veda,' then must the pupil, taking the second step, ponder over them and try to understand them and have them demonstrated to him by reasoning. For, to be satisfied merely with hearing, would mean nothing more than vague beliefs. That his beliefs may be transformed into rational and logical convictions, he must consider all the arguments, first against, and then for, the statements. And then weighing both, must come to rational conclusions about them.

But here again, if he were to do this by himself unaided, the chances are he would go astray and would probably never be able to come to a right conclusion at all. So the Ṛiṣhis, ever desirous to help man, again come forward and show the line of reasoning which may be pursued. Thus did the Ṛiṣhis, Kaṇâda and Gotama,

---

* Nyâ. Sû., Bhâṣh., Nyâ. Vâr., IV ii 47; Prashasta, pp. 281 and 282; Kandalî, p. 282; Upask., Vivṛ. IV. ii. 16; Saptap. and Mit., p. 32, &c., &c.

teach. They pointed out to, and established for, deserving pupils the lines of reasoning which show *how* the 'statements' of the truths must be true, that is to say, how they can be demonstrated.*

And it is these lines of reasoning, as founded by Kaṇâda and Gotama, which constitute philosophy, *i.e.*, the Vaisheṣhika and the Nyâya.†

Philosophy as reasoning and metaphysical truth.

Thus philosophy is *not* reasoning and speculation with a view to *discover* metaphysical truths, but it is reasoning with a view to logically *demonstrate* and *understand* these truths which are already *given* as facts of experience, and as propositions enunciated in the 'Words of the Veda.'‡

Philosophy and Speculation.

Reasoning and speculation about transcendental, *i.e.*, metaphysical truths, not already given as experienced facts, can never do more than lead us to a probability. But as often they mislead us.§ Then again, there is no certainty in reasoning as a means of discovering transcendental truths. What one clever man to-day establishes as true by mere reasoning, another cleverer man demolishes to-morrow as devoid of foundation. Mere reasoning, therefore, cannot lead us to certainty about transcendental and metaphysical truths. Reasoning is merely a means of understanding them. And because it is this kind of reasoning which, as stated before, constitutes philosophy, (as the Hindus understand it) the latter is also only a *means* of understanding, not discovering, truths.

---

* Ki. Va., p. 4. † Upask., Intro., pp. 2 and 3 ; Vivṛ., Intro., p. 2 and V. ii. 16. (Intro). ‡ *See* Note 57. § *See* Note 58.

This being so, the object of philosophy—as understood by the ancient teachers of India—is *not* the mere solution of an intellectual problem for its own sake—not the mere performance of intellectual gymnastics, with no better result than just the sharpening of the reasoning faculties, and as often the perverting of them.* On the contrary, the object of philosophy is to aid *suffering* man to understand truth which is put before him, so that, by understanding it, he may afterwards realise it; and by the realisation of truth may become free and thus end his sorrows and sufferings. Thus philosophy is one of the most practical of all practical things, inasmuch as it is a means to the gaining of an end which is the highest that man can conceive. For this end, on the road to which philosophy is a step, is no other than true freedom, absolute independence. Philosophy is the middle step to the gaining of this end.

Object of Philosophy.

This middle or second step of the Hindu in acquiring philosophic truths may be compared to that step of Euclid which is called 'demonstration' in regard to geometrical truths.

The third and final step is Realisation by direct experience. It is technically called Samâdhi, or more generally, Yoga. And it is by this last step, that truth is really acquired and made one's own.† The first gives it merely as a matter of faith, the second turns it into a rational conviction,

Third Step. Realisation of metaphysical truths by direct experience—Yoga.

---

* *See* Note 59.

† Nyâ. Sû., IV. ii. 38; IV. ii. 46. *Supra.* *See* Note 60.

but the third alone gives the truth by experience. Neither merely hearsay knowledge, rather information, about truth, nor merely intellectual and inferential conviction in regard to it, can possibly make us free and end our sufferings. Such information and inference are knowledge only in a secondary sense—knowledge which is indirect and theoretical. And no merely theoretical knowledge can possibly end so actual a thing as human suffering is. It is, therefore, the realisation of truth by direct experience which is the only *radical* remedy of the ills of specific existences—the only way to freedom. And, to repeat, it is this realisation which the third step, Yoga, secures.

Yoga and philosophy proper.

But with Yoga we pass beyond the limits of philosophy proper—philosophy which is, from the Hindu point of view, only the monstration, by reasoning, of propositions enunciating transcendental or metaphysical truths.

A few of the main principles of Yoga.

To explain fully what Yoga really is and how it can lead to direct experience of the metaphysical truths would mean a separate detreatise by itself. Here we can just touch upon a few of its main principles.

We find that we are aware of things by directing our minds, that is, by paying attention, to them. The greater the attention the more is our awareness of things. On the other hand, if we can withdraw our minds and attention altogether from a thing, it is not perceived at all, even if it be before us all the time.

That this is true in regard to things physical we all more or less know. But that it is true in regard to things mental also, is not perhaps so obvious. Yet many of us know that by concentrating our minds on any problem or puzzle, as much as on a physical thing, we can often have it solved as though in a flash. That such acquisition of knowledge by concentrating our minds on things mental is possible, all discoverers and inventors will probably bear testimony to.

Experiences of this kind would seem to indicate, that if we could concentrate our minds on anything *to perfection*, we might perhaps know all about it. I say we *might* perhaps know all about a thing. The Hindus maintain that we can *certainly* know everything by this means. For, it is after all the mind (Manas) which is the direct and immediate instrument of all experience and awareness. The senses merely assist it in its operation. But this assistance of the senses is not absolutely indispensable. It *is* indeed indispensable as long as the mind is not able to work, as it were, on its own account. But once it is able to do this, it can bring about knowledge and experience of things *without* the help of the senses.

Such possibilities of the human mind would certainly not be admitted by the vast majority of people in the West. But even scientific men in the West are beginning to turn their attention to the study of such phenomena as hypnotism, which is now recognised practically by everybody as a fact, and telepathy which some at least regard as proved to be true. These, however, are phenomena which, in the opinion of the Hindus, are only of a most elementary character and just the indications of what the human mind is capable of doing. With further studies along these lines, say the Hindus, the West may perhaps change its opinion and see, that not only in a few abnormal cases and within narrow limits can the mind of man bring knowledge and experience of things without the intervention of the senses, but that it can do so habitually and in all things. But before the mind can do this, say they, one must learn to concentrate it on anything to perfection.

Whatever the West may think about it, practically the whole of the East, where Hindu thought, including Buddhism, has had any influence, is of one opinion in this matter.* Both the Hindus and Buddhists, who have devoted themselves to the cultivation of it from early times, maintain that concentration of the mind can be practised to absolute perfection, and that, when perfected, by its means alone everything can be known and realised as direct experience.

Yoga or Samâdhi is perfected concentration.

And it is this perfected power of concentration, enabling a man to realise everything by direct experience, which they call Yoga (or Samâdhi.)

Yoga is a combination of absolute calmness and most penetrating keenness.

But when concentration is perfect, say these people, then the mind becomes absolutely still, like a flame in a place where there is not even the gentlest breath of wind.‡ The simile of the flame in this connection is significant. It means that the mind, when thus concentrated and stilled is not dull and sleepy, but fully alive and most keenly penetrating.†

---

* *See* Note 61.

‡ *See* Note 62. Bhag. Gîtâ, vi. 19.

Only, in this state, the mind has not the slightest flicker in it. Thus it is a combination of *keenness* and *stillness* and not the dead dull state of a stone.

Yoga is no idleness.

Being a combination of these two apparently contradictory aspects, it is obvious that the concentration desired cannot be gained by idleness or by anything that would throw the mind into a dull state.*

It can be achieved only by combining in one's life and character those two things which can, on the one hand, sharpen the mental faculties and, on the other, quiet the heart. It is obvious that the sharpening and developing of the faculties of the mind is possible only if we exercise them ; and we can exercise them, again, only if we bring them into activity by doing something that requires thought or by thinking out some problem, that is to say, by conducting ourselves so as to develop thoughtfulness in us.

Yoga is impossible by leading selfish life.

But this conduct, leading to thoughtfulness and development of mental faculties, is *generally* followed with some personal motive and personal interest, as distinguished from, and considered as opposed to, the interests of others. That is to say, it is followed with what may be called a selfish motive, with Ahaṅkâra, as it is called in Sanskrit. But as long as any selfish interest is the motive of conduct, that conduct can never give us the stillness and quiet which must be combined with keenness. By following such a conduct with selfish motives, one can no doubt develop keenness. But together with keenness there

* *See* Note 63.

will always be disturbance in the mind, because the man, following such a course, will always have thoughts and feelings like : "oh, this is mine ; I must have this ; somebody will perhaps get in my way ; I must fight him," and so on. All these thoughts and ideas breed passions in our hearts ; and when the passions rage, no stillness is ever possible.

How the would-be Yogin should live.

To have, therefore, both absolute calmness and keenness of the mind, a man must so conduct himself in life as to do all he can to develop his mental faculties and keenness, but with a motive which is absolutely impersonal or selfless.* The only way to accomplish this is to do faithfully and thoughtfully all that is really a man's duty in life, and to do these duties *as duties* simply, without permitting oneself to think of what advantage can be personally gained by the doing of them. Nor should a man permit himself to be so entangled in thought and care about the duty that he can never put it off his mind and that it intrudes itself upon him even when the day's work is done and he wants to think of something else. The doing of one's real duties in this spirit will bring all one's faculties into play and exercise and thus develop them ; and as they develop, the mind will grow in keenness—one of the requisites of concentration. Such living will also eliminate from the heart all cause of disturbance, by gradually expunging from it all notions and feelings of personal and selfish interests, all thought of 'I' and 'me' and 'mine' as opposed to 'you' and 'yours' or 'he' and 'his.'

---

* *See* Note 64.

These thoughts and feelings will never find any nourishment in a man if he keeps himself busy with duty which is done simply as duty and without any thought of personal gain or advantage. And when thoughts and feelings of personal interests are gone and therewith all cause of disturbance is removed, the heart is free from passions and therefore full of calm—the second requisite of concentration.

Thus by doing duty, as duty, and without getting entangled in it, a man can gradually develop in himself the two indispensable and yet apparently contradictory requirements of concentration. There is no other way by which this can be done, for all other ways will develop either keenness, *with* selfishness —with the thought 'I,' 'me' and 'mine;' or, stillness *without* keenness, which is only dulness and stupidity.

This mode of living or conduct without any selfish interest and entanglement in it is technically called Karma-Yoga. It may be practised in various ways, but those cannot be very well explained here. All that we need to understand, for our present purpose, is simply the principle that, in order to develop both keenness and stillness together, a man must begin by living, not an idle life, but an active life, doing all that is needful and all that is duty, but only *as* duty with an absolutely unselfish motive, and without any entanglement in it. That is to say, he must aim at being well-nigh perfect in moral character. For, if a man can eliminate from his nature all thought of personal interest as opposed to the interests of others, and, therefore, all thought of personal gratification which may lead to the harming of any living being or to the feeding of any passions in himself, he cannot but be morally perfect.

The foundation of Yoga—perfection in moral life.

This is the one indispensable pre-requisite, and the very foundation of Yoga which leads to direct experience of metaphysical truths. It is no good talking of Yoga until this is practised, at any rate to a great extent.* And when this is done to a large extent, a man is fit for practical concentration, which then becomes comparatively easy.

Secondary helps in Yoga.

And to practise concentration when the preliminary qualification is gained, the man may take advantage of certain secondary aids.† Of these there are several; but perhaps only two need be mentioned here. These are :—

(i) The regulation of diet so as to keep the body in such a state that it may not produce any feelings of dulness, stupidity or heaviness on the one hand, or too much restlessness on the other; that it may be, as it were, a most delicate and sensitive instrument, and in perfect health, *if possible.*

(ii) Seclusion, occasional if not permanent, from the hurry and bustle of life, in a pleasant spot, such as a quiet river bank with beautiful scenery, or a mountain, forest dale, and so on.

In such a spot, seating himself in a position which will be easy and comfortable, so that the body may not disturb or distract the mind by its discomfort on the

---

* *See* Note 65.

† Nyā. Sū., IV. II. 42.

one hand, nor send it to sleep on the other, the man should try to fix his thought on any object of which he wants to know the truth.

When he succeeds in fixing his thought absolutely,

Some results of Yoga.

he will know all that there is to know about it, He will, for instance, come to realise* :—

(*a*) That the things consist of Paramâṇus ; he will know this by becoming actually aware of the Paramâṇus by means of his mind.

(*b*) That Âkâsha and the other Realities exist. These he will realise by similarly becoming aware of them.

(*c*) That the Âtman is not the same as the body. This will be realised by separating his mind from the body, and thereby withdrawing his whole being from it as 'the soft blade is drawn out of a grass' or as 'a sword is drawn from its sheath,' or as 'a snake draws itself out from its skin.'

When he can do this he knows how experience can be had *without* the body.

(*d*) That man is born and dies again and again. This will be realised by remembering all his past lives and by being actually aware of the fact that when a man dies in one place, that which constituted his inner life in the body that is dead re-appears somewhere else.

By realising the truth of Re-incarnation and by remembering all his past lives he also realises all the

* *See* Note 66.

Adṛishṭa which lies behind him and may lead him to other births.* And as he knows these Adṛishṭas he meets and counteracts them in a way, which, the Hindus hold, there is, and which gives everyone his due, so that all justice is done. It is in this way that all the *waiting* Adṛishṭas are exhausted.

(*e*) That there are worlds and beings which are never perceived by the senses. This, again, is realised by being actually aware of them.

In this way he may realise all the facts and principles pertaining to the transcendental, that is, the supersensible, and may finally realise *himself*, that is to say, the Âtman, as separate from, and independent of, everything else. When this is done he no longer feels that he is the body or the mind. With this realisation, all identification of himself in thought and desire with any specific form of existence ceases and the man is free.

This then is briefly Yoga, which constitutes the third step in the method of acquiring and realising philosophical truths.

Unlike the first two, this third step in the Hindu method of acquiring metaphysical truths, has no actual parallel in Euclidean geometry. But if to the two steps already named, *i.e.*, Enunciation and Demonstration, a third could be added, namely, Verification of the truth of the propositions established by reasoning, then the same might be said to correspond to the third step of this Hindu metaphysical method, that is to say, to Yoga.

* Nyâ. Bhâṣh., IV. i. 64; Prashasta, p. 281 (bottom); Upask., V. ii. 18; VI. ii. 16.

Thus, for instance, if the proposition, that three angles of a triangle are equal to two right angles, as an enunciation, corresponds to the first step of the Hindu metaphysical method, and the demonstration of this proposition by reasoning corresponds to the second step, or philosophy proper as understood by the Hindus, then there might be added a third step corresponding to the Yoga of the Hindus. This step would be something like the following. Suppose, that after demonstrating the proposition, or having it demonstrated to him, a man takes a piece of paper and cuts it into a triangular shape; and measuring the angles, he finds that they make exactly 180 degrees. Such a procedure in regard to a geometrical truth, giving him direct knowledge or realisation of what was already learnt by reasoning, might be said, *in a way only,** to correspond to Yoga in the matter of transcendental truths.

The pupil becomes the teacher.

When, following Yoga, the learner realises the truths by direct experience, he himself becomes a Ṛiṣhi, a freed man and a teacher in his turn.

Conclusion.

Such then is the Realism which the Hindus teach to those not capable of understanding *by reasoning* the psycho-dynamic or polyonymic presentation of the true nature of things. But even a candidate, not intellectually qualified or temperamentally inclined to follow the presentations of the other Standards, can reach the same goal as any others, when, by practice, he comes

* *See* Note 67 and Appendix C.

to realise the truths as presented by Realism.* This goal, as said so often, is the absolute freedom and independence of the Real in man ; it is freedom from all sorrow and suffering, and, above all, from every *necessity* and *compulsion*, and is gained by freeing oneself from the one and only prolific source of all other necessities, —the necessity and compulsion to be born in a specific form of existence. And he can reach this goal even without realising what may be called the secondary things, such as the ultimate nature of the Paramâṇus, Âkâsha and so on ; that is to say, whether they be really eternal and everlasting or are derived things, or whether there be really many Âtmans or only one.†

For, as already indicated, to realise the goal, that is, absolute freedom, all that he needs is that he should no longer be prompted to activity with a view to gain some advantage to himself as opposed to others, and, to this end, to be absolutely free from likes and dislikes, special attachment for some things and aversion for others. When these latter cease, a man no longer hankers after some things as specially desired or seeks to avoid others as undesirable. And this object is gained the moment it is realised that all the diverse forms of things, which hitherto appeared variously as beautiful or hideous, as attractive or repulsive, are but groups of Paramâṇus that are all alike. Suppose a man could, by an extraordinary power akin to, say, that of the ideally perfect microscope, see things so magnified that they appeared to him as nothing but a swirling mass of particles which were all alike, it is obvious he could

---

* *See* Note 68

† *See* Note 69.

not be specially drawn by any one of them; and ceasing to be drawn by any of them, he would not be repelled either by others. Similarly, when a man realises *by experience*, and is not merely convinced by reasoning, that all perceptible things are but Paramâṇus which are all alike, he cannot possibly have any likes or dislikes for any of them. Once this is realised, it matters little whether he knows them further as eternally existing or as derived things.

Then again in regard to the Âtman, the moment a man realises this as himself by experience, and not merely as an intellectual conviction, he ceases to have special attachment for any specific form of embodiment, human or superhuman. And ceasing to have special attachment for any particular forms, he is not repelled by others. Thus he is again free from likes and dislikes and all that they imply. This freedom from likes and dislikes by the realisation of himself as the Âtman is further strengthened by this other experience in regard to the forms of embodiments themselves, the experience, namely, that they are, like all other discrete things, themselves but masses of Paramâṇus, which are all alike.

Thus, by just realising oneself as the Âtman, one can realise the desired end without further enquiring whether the Âtman which is himself is the only one in the Universe or whether there are others. Nor will this mean any limitation to the Âtman which is himself, or make any *practical* difference. For the Âtman, being infinite in nature, and without any distinguishing features which may differentiate it from other Âtmans (supposing there are such), will realise itself, as a matter of fact, as one with them all, in their character as pure Âtman, *i.e.*, as not associated with particular Adṛiṣhṭas and embodiments.

Thus, without enquiring further into the ultimate character of the Paramâṇus, Âkâsha, Kâla and Dik, and Manases as eternal Realities or derived things or intothe question of the oneness or plurality of Âtmans, and by just realising the truths as presented by Realism, the Realist can reach the same goal as the others.

When the goal is realised, the Realist may or may not care to know what I have called secondary things. If he does, after the nine classes of Realities as taught by his own Standard are realised as existing facts, he may perhaps also know them as the other Standards teach them to be. But if he does not care to pursue his enquiries further in this direction, he may still hold these as eternal verities. But in any case, as far as the ultimate goal and main object is concerned, he gains it by following the path of Realism, just as much as those whose intellectual reasoning even did not stop at that point of the analysis of things where the nine Realities of Realism were discovered as facts. Thus Realism, like the other systems, serves the same purpose, and it has, like them, ever been studied in India as a means, an intermediate means, to the gaining of the one supreme end, namely, Absolute Freedom, *i.e.*, Mokṣha or Mukti. Realism, therefore, like the other metaphysical systems of the Hindus, has a most practical aim and object in view.

NOTES.

1 (p. 2). That the philosophy of the Hindus, *i.e.*, the original Darshana Shâstra, consists only of rational demonstration of propositions laid down in the Vedas is clear from the following extracts :—

(*a*) Shâstran-tu ṣhaḍ-vidham : Vaisheṣhika-Nyâya-Mîmâṁsâ-Sâṅkhya - Pâtañjala - rûpam. Etâni tattva-jñânârtham Vedân vichârya Kaṇâda-Gotama-Jaimini-Kapila - Patañjali- Vedavyâsâ-khyair muni-ṣhaṭkaih kṛitâni (Sha. ka., *sub voce* Darshana).

(*b*) Veda-viṣhaya-nirṇayâyaiva utpannam sumahat Darshana-Shâstram. (Sa. Sâ. Ni., Vol. IV, p. ne, line 1).

That the notion of the Hindus in regard to their own philosophy is as embodied in the above extracts has been admitted even by Mr. N. Shastri Goreh. And his admission is very significant as he was, being a Christian convert an opponent of the Hindus. He says :—

"Of these (*i.e.*, Darshanas) the staple is argument. But they profess to derive their views from the Veda and other sacred books. Independent authority as to those views they disclaim."

—Goreh, *Ration. Refut.*, p. 1.

2 (p. 2). The name Darshana, which is now in common use, seems originally to have meant not so much a complete system of views as any particular view or doctrine. And in this sense it is often replaced by Dṛiṣhṭi, which

means the same thing. *See* Nyâ. Bhâṣh., I. i. 23; III. ii. 35; IV. i. 14; Nyâ. Vâr., IV. i. 14, &c.

Both these words occur in their Pâli forms in the same senses in the Buddhist Suttas, *i.e.*, "Discourses of the Buddha." *See* Sâleyyaka-Sutta (41)., Maj. Nik., I. v. 1., p. 288 of Vol. I, Pâli Text. Soc.'s edition.

As for the two other current names, Manana Shâstra and Vichâra Shâstra, *see* Cha. Kâ., Vol. I, p. 102; Vivṛ., VI. ii. 16.

While these three names, Darshana-, Manana-, and Vichâra-Shâstra, will be recognised by everybody as being used in these days, the more ancient names seem to have been some of those words which are now used in specific and restrictive senses, *i.e.*, not meaning philosophy generally. These are:—

Mîmâṁsâ or Mîmâṁsâ-Shâstra,
Tarka or Tarka-Shâstra,
Ânvîkṣhikî,
and
Nyâya-Vidyâ.

See, for instance, the Commentary by Râghavânanda on Manu, XII. 106, where both the words Mîmâṁsâ and Tarka have been used in the sense of general philosophy and not in the special senses in which they are now used. *See* also the Viveka on the Tantrâloka of Abhinava Gupta (i. 10.) As for Ânvîkṣhikî, *see* Shabdakalpadruma, *sub voce*, where it is explained as Adhyâtma-vidyâ.

Finally, Nyâya, although now used almost exclusively as a name of the system founded by Gotama, originally does not seem to mean anything more than mere reasoning, as for instance, in Nyâya-Vârttika, IV. i. 14. That it meant general reasoning, and not specifically Gotama's Philosophy, is also clear from the fact that in the Nyâya-Sûchî by Vâchaspati Mishra, the section on syllogism only, namely, Sûtras, I. 1, 32-39, is spoken of as Nyâya-Prakaraṇa. *See* Nyâya-Sûchî, published in the Bib. Ind. as an Appendix to Fas. IV. of Nyâya-Vârttika. That Nyâya meant Philosophy generally is evident also from the fact that it is used as part of the name of such works as the Nyâyamâla-Vistara, which is a work not on the Nyâya-Darshana, as it is now understood, but on the Karma-Mîmâṁsâ.

3 (p.6). The pre-conceptions of the Hindus given here are not mentioned in so many words in any one particular place. But they can be easily gathered from their various writings. *See*, for instance, Cha. Kâ., Vol. I, p. 6. and Vol. V, pp. 32-181. Also Goreh, p. 1, para. 2.

4 (p. 6). A Ṛiṣhi need not *necessarily* be a 'perfected seer,' *i.e.*, a 'Freed Man' (Mukta-Puruṣha). There may be Ṛiṣhis who are 'seers' not only of lower things but of a transcendental nature. Such Ṛiṣhis may strive after perfect and final wisdom and then be freed. *See* Shâr. Bhâṣh., I. iii. 26. But of course the Ṛiṣhis who are the founders of the Darshana must be regarded as "perfected seers," because they are all Mukta-Puruṣhas.

5 (p. 7). The existing Sûtras may be much later than the Ṛiṣhis themselves. What is meant by saying that the Ṛiṣhis are the founders of the systems is that they are the founders of the lines of arguments and the standards, not necessarily the writers of the current works. In corroboration of the statement that the systems may be

much older than the existing Sûtras the following may be quoted :—

"It is necessary, however, to state that in appealing to the Sâṅkhya, I appeal to the doctrine and not to the text-books. There is abundant evidence, both in Hindu and Buddhist works of unquestionable antiquity and authenticity, of the Sâṅkhya and Yoga systems having been current before the time of Buddha."

Preface to "Aphor. of Patañjali," being Trans. of Yoga Sûtras (p. xvi) by Râjâ Râjendralâl Mitra.

6 (p. 13). That the Paramâṇus of the Vaisheṣhika are not rejected by the Sâṅkhya but are accepted as derived things under the name of Tanmâtras will be seen from Gauḍ. Sâṅkh. 22. *See* however Bhâṣhya on Yoga Sûtra, III. 43, with Vyâkhyâ of Vâchaspati and Yoga Vârttika of Vijñâna-Bhikṣhu on it.

As for the other principles of Realism, it is well known they are all recognised by the Sâṅkhya, but not as finalities, except the Âtmans. The Âtmans even are conceived differently. *See* further Note 37.

7 (p. 17). In connection with the remark that the "ideas (nâma-rûpa)......are *under no circumstances* part of the one and absolute Reality," it has to be noticed that there is an interpretation of the Vedânta, *i.e.*, the Upaniṣhads, which *does* consider these as part of the Real, that is, Brahman. This interpretation is now represented by Râmânuja and his School though it was not originated by him. But even Dr. Thibaut, who is inclined to think that Râmânuja interprets the meaning of the Brahma-Sûtras more faithfully than Shaṅkara, cannot but admit the fact that it is the latter

who has a greater claim, than Râmânuja, to being the right interpreter of the Upanishads, *i.e.*, the real and original Vedânta. *See* Preface to his translation of the Shâr. Bhâsh. in the "Sacred Books of the East," under the title of the Vedânta Sûtras, Vol. I, pp. cxxii, *et seq.* *See* specially lines 13, &c., on p. cxxiv.

And it is according to Shankara's interpretation of the Vedânta that the above statement is made.

It is a very difficult and extensive subject and cannot possibly be fully treated here.

8 (p. 19). In regard to the Paramânus, the Nyâya-Vaisheshika holds the following ideas :—

A Paramânu is—

(*a*) absolutely without any magnitude. Its measure is anu, which is not the lowest *degree* of magnitude, *i.e.*, a measure consisting of length, breadth and thickness, however minute, but is of a *totally opposite* character. *See* Vaish. Sû., VII. i. 10. (The reading of this Sûtra in Gangâ. is 'Mahato viparîtam anu,' the other reading being 'Ato viparî., etc.'); Ki. Va. Pr., quoted in Ki. Va., p. 52; Roer, note on Bhâshâ Par. 14 (but marked 15); also Intro., pp. x-xi; Banerjea, Dial. Phil., 158-159, &c.,

(*b*) non-spatial. Nyâ. Vâr., IV. ii. 25, p. 522, line 3,

(*c*) has no inside or outside. Nyâ. Sû., IV. ii. 20, with Bhâsh. and Vâr.,

(*d*) is super-sensible and can be conceived only by the mind. Nyâ. Vâr., p. 233, &c.; N. V. T. T., p. 271, line 7 from bottom, &c.

(*e*) The measure of the Paramâṇus, being added up, cannot produce any magnitude or any other measure because they are absolutely without any magnitude. Upask., VII. ii. 9, &c., &c.; Sid. Mu. Va. on 14.

In these circumstances it is very misleading to call Paramâṇus 'atoms' as has hitherto been done. This rendering of Paramâṇus is responsible in no small degree for the almost contemptuous attitude with which some European scholars have looked upon the Vaisheṣhika.

What the Vaisheṣhika has emphasised is not so much the 'uncutability' of the Paramâṇus as their measure, which is the very *opposite* of magnitude. Aṇu means their measure, whereas whoever invented the name 'atom' had probably the idea of its indivisibility more than anything else in his mind.

The Paramâṇus are not unlike the 'qualitative atoms' of Herbart and his School, in so far as these latter are the bases of things material. But it is perhaps much better to leave the Sanskrit word untranslated.

9 (p. 20). The word Power or Force as a translation of Shakti is meant to convey the idea of an independent Reality and not that of the *capacity* of a thing, such as the '*capacity* of fire to burn.' Shakti in the latter sense is never regarded as an independent Reality by the Vaisheṣhika. But that Shakti can be used in the former sense will be seen from Cha. Kâ., Vol. II, p. 151, where Âtman is spoken of as a sort of Shakti. (Shakti-visheṣha.)

10 (p. 22). I use the phrase 'purely subjective dream' as a translation of Svapna to distinguish it from

what is called Svapnântika. This latter word is used by some to denote those dreams which are something like prophetic. The existence of such dreams is regarded by the Hindus as a fact. *See* Vaish. Sû., IX. ii. 7 and 8, with Upask. and Vivṛ.

11 (p. 25-27). The line of argument followed here is based, as will be seen from the references, on authoritative Nyâya-Vaisheṣhika Texts. Nor need it be supposed that I have been influenced by Herbart and Lotze. For I knew nothing of Herbart and Lotze when I learned the interpretation given here.

The argument based on the idea that divisibility must stop somewhere, otherwise there is no reason why Mount Meru and a mustard seed should be so different in size, as well as certain other arguments, seem to be of later origin. There is hardly any trace of them in the Sûtras or even in Prashastapâda's work which has been regarded as the mine (Âkara) of information on the Vaisheṣhika by all subsequent writers on the subject. Shrîdhara in his Kandalî does not allude to it either.

12 (p. 29). The idea which I have had in my mind when speaking of 'a thing of the nature of a line' is that of a dvyaṇuka, hitherto translated by 'binary,' in agreement with the translation of Paramâṇus by 'atoms.' But I have stated before my objection to this latter translation. A dvyaṇuka, produced by two Paramâṇus, which are like mathematical points, can be only a thing of the nature of a line—the shortest possible line. It is distinctly stated that the *measure* a dvyaṇuka has is produced by the dvitva or duality of two Paramâṇus perceived *as dual*. That is to say, it is produced by

two Paramâṇus which must be so placed that they can be recognised as two (dvitvasya...*apekṣhâ-buddhi*-janyasya kâraṇatvam ; Upask., VII. i. 10). This perception of the two Paramâṇus, producing a dvyaṇuka, as *two* entities would be impossible if they were not placed apart from one another. And if two Paramâṇus which are like mathematical points produce a thing by being placed thus, it is obvious the produced thing can be only a thing of the nature of a line.

A dvyaṇuka is regarded as a thing which by itself can never be perceived by the senses, which is quite natural. For a line by itself is certainly imperceptible.

Three of these dvyaṇukas again produce the tryaṇuka or trasareṇu which is a thing *with magnitude.*

But it is not maintained that *only three* of the dvyaṇukas can combine together. Kandalî says clearly that *any other number* can certainly combine and produce various other forms. But *no magnitude, i.e.,* length, breadth and thickness, can be produced by a *less number* of dvyaṇukas than three. (*See* Kandalî, p. 32, lines 6 *et seq.*) This, too, is quite obvious, for never can a magnitude having length, breadth and thickness be produced by a less number of lines than three.

As for the idea that a tryaṇuka or trasareṇu is 'like a mote in the sunbeam,' it is a later one. We do not find it either in the Sûtras or in other early works. Even if this were a notion held by the founders of the system, it would hardly make any difference in their position. This position is, it may be repeated, that Paramâṇus are things without magnitude, non-spatial and so on; that they first relate themselves together in twos; that these latter combine in numbers *not less* than three, and that, when they so combine, magnitude is produced.

Perhaps one possible objection against my rendering of dvyaṇuka as a thing of the nature of the shortest possible line would be that the measure of a dvyaṇuka is also spoken of as aṇu, though it is regarded as a produced measure. But we must remember that, in the first place, this application of the term aṇu to the measure of a dvyaṇuka is a later one. Secondly, aṇu in this sense means only a measure which is not mahat, *i.e.*, magnitude, and is yet super-sensible in the same sense as a Paramâṇu is super-sensible (*see* ante, p. 54). That this is the meaning of aṇutva (*i.e.*, aṇu-ness) as applied to a dvyaṇuka is quite clear from both Upask. and Vivṛ. on VII. i. 10.

Thirdly, there is a clear distinction made between the aṇutva of a dvyaṇuka and that of a Paramâṇu. The aṇutva of a Paramâṇu is pârimâṇḍalya, *i.e.*, without any elongation whatever, whereas the measure of a dvyaṇuka is never pârimâṇḍalya. (Prashasta, p. 130, last two lines). This is significant. For it implies that a dvyaṇuka is not a parimaṇḍala but a something which has elongation, *i.e.*, is a line.

13 (p. 31). The arguments given here and in the following two paragraphs are only the applications of certain general principles recognised by Nyâya-Vaish. They are based on Vaish. Sû., II. i. 13 ; Nyâya-Bhâṣh., IV. ii. 22 (latter part) ; Nyâ. Mañj., p. 502, line 5 (from bottom), and so on.

14 (p. 32). This is based on those arguments of the Nyâya-Vaisheṣhika whereby it is shown how even a

Truṭi, *i.e.*, a thing of the smallest magnitude, cannot be final. *See*, for instance, Nyâ. Vâr., II. i. 33, p. 234, line 3, with N. V. T. Ṭ., on it; the passage in Nyâ. Mañj. referred to in Note 13 and so on.

15 (p. 32). This argument is based on Nyâ. Sû., IV. ii. 19, where it is given as a Pûrva-Pakṣha, *i.e.*, an objection which can be valid only if the ultimate particles are regarded as things *with* magnitude.

16 (p. 35). The Sanskrit word which I have rendered here as 'temperature' is Sparsha. It has been hitherto translated as 'touch' to the great disadvantage of Hindu Realism. Sparsha as a quality is distinctly stated to be only of three kinds, namely, hot, cold, and neither-hot-nor-cold. It is also added that 'hardness, softness' and the like are *not* forms of Sparsha but are forms of contact (Saṁyoga-visheṣhâḥ). In these circumstances it is misleading to translate Sparsha by touch. *See* Prashasta, p. 102, with Kandalî on it. Nyâ. Bhâṣh., III. i. 56 and 57; N. V. T. Ṭ., p. 150, line 3 (from bottom); Tarkasaṅgraha, p. 16; &c., &c.

17 (p. 38). The definition given here of Âpaḥ is based on similar ones of the three other Bhûtas. The Lakṣhaṇâvalî gives it differently.

18 (p. 42). The Nyâya-Vaisheṣhika regards the Paramâṇus as constituting the four classes given here. But of course the *way* in which the classification is *explained* here is my own.

19 (p. 45). My reasons for calling the sense by means of which Sparsha is perceived, the temperature-sense, are the same as those mentioned in Note 16. If

Sparsha is temperature, then the sense by which it is perceived is also the temperature-sense.

20 (pp. 47 and 60). In all the later works on Nyâya-Vaish., the existence of Âkâsha is supported exclusively on the ground of its being the basis of sound. The opening Sûtra of Kaṇâda of the section on Âkâsha (Vaish. Sû., III. i. 20) is now regarded as expressing a view which is that of the Sâṅkhyas. This Sûtra says that we must admit the existence of Âkâsha because there must be a medium to supply room for the discrete sensible things to move about (sañchâra, according to both Upask. and Vivṛ. The Sûtra itself says 'coming out and going in.') This reason, however, say the two commentaries named above, is set aside by Kaṇâda in the next Sûtra. This interpretation seems doubtful and may have originated with the author of Upask. Shaṅkara Mishra wrote the Upask. relying only on the Sûtras as he himself tells us (introductory verse 3); and it is not unlikely that much of his interpretation is only his own invention. That his interpretation of the section on Âkâsha is his own there is reason to suspect. Târkika-Rakṣhâ, which is an older work than Upask., seems to take the opening Sûtra as embodying not the view of the Sâṅkhya but of the Vaisheṣhika itself. (Târ. Rak., p. 123). Chandra-Kânta in his Bhâṣhya also takes the same view. (Chan. Bhâṣh. on II. i. 20 *et seq.*)

The only serious objection to the interpretation of Târ. Rak. and Chan. Bhâṣh. being correct is that Nyâ-Vâr. also maintains that the existence of Âkâsha can be maintained only on the ground of its being the basis of sound. Nyâ. Vâr., III. i. 72, p. 400.

On the other hand Nyâya-Vaish., like the other systems, refers constantly to Âkâsha as the room and locality, one of the supports (âdhâra), if not the only support, of all discrete things; Ki. Va., p. 35; Kandalî, p. 22 (line 10 from bottom); Prashasta speaks of all the other Bhûtas as existing in Âkâsha (pp. 48 last line to p. 49, line 7).

Thus it would seem that Târ. Rak. and Chan. Bhâṣh. are quite right in taking the Sûtra, II. i. 20, as setting forth the view of the Vaisheṣhika itself.

This conclusion would be greatly strengthened if we could rely on the reading of the Sûtras as given by Gaṅgâdhara in his edition of the Vaisheṣhika. He reads the Sûtra, II. i. 5, as 'Ta âkâshe vidyante,' instead of 'Ta âkâshe na vidyante.' And he seems to interpret it as follows:—Those objective things (Te viṣhayâḥ) exist in Âkâsha.—(Gaṅgâ., p. 42).

For all these reasons I have given two lines of argument in support of Âkâsha instead of only the usual Shabdâdhâratva or Shabdâshrayatva (sound-supportingness) of most of the later Vaisheṣhika works.

In any case the arguments given in here are quite in harmony with and based on authoritative texts.

21 (p. 48). The all-pervasiveness of Âkâsha is often supported on other grounds. The arguments given here are based on what is called Dharmigrâhaka-pramâṇa, *i.e.*, an argument which proves at once both the existence and characteristic of a thing, like the one proving the existence of Manas or of Kâla, as well as their nature. Part of the argument is also what is called 'lâghava,' *i.e.*, that of the simplest theory. *See* Nyâ. Vṛit. on IV.

i. 28, where eternity of Âkâsha is said to be so established (dharmigrâhaka-mânena lâghava-sahakṛitena).

22 (p. 54). Jñâna, *i.e.*, consciousness or even experience, is spoken of as dravya. If consciousness can be called substance, then dravya is substance. *See* Shrî-Bhâṣh., II. ii. 27, p. 1573.

23 (p. 55). One of the reasons why there has been so much misunderstanding in regard to Kâla is that it has been taken to be Time in the Western sense of the word. That Kâla is the great power which whirls things round is a common Hindu notion. *See*, for instance, Viṣh. Pur., I. i.

24 (p. 56). This seems to be a very old argument. It is given by Vâchaspati Mishra in N. V. T. Ṭ., p. 280. Udayana also quotes it in Ki. Va. and attributes it to an Âchârya. This Âchârya, we are told by Vardhamâna, is Vyoma-Shiva (Ki. Va., p. 114). Udayana thinks it defective as stated by Vyoma-Shiva. But he does not seem to discard it altogether. For he says that Kâla, Dik and Manas must be conceived as without any 'special qualities' by virtue of dharmigrâhaka-pramâṇa (Ki. Va., p. 110). He could not possibly have urged this as a reason if he discarded the old argument attributed by him to Vyoma-Shiva.

Nowhere that I know of is this argument stated in any but the curtest form, almost unintelligible to any but those taught orally by the Hindus themselves. The common form of it is simply 'Visheṣhaguṇavattvât.'

25 (pp. 59-60). Like Kâla, Dik has been much misunderstood. That Dik is a power which *holds* things in various *positions* is a common Hindu idea. This power

is often spoken of as the 'Elephants of the quarters' that hold up the world *in space*, or as divine maids that uphold creation. It is also spoken of as the arms that support and uphold things. *See* Nîlakaṇṭha on Ma. Bhâr., I. lxiv. 38; Ma. Bhâr. III. cc. (*i.e.* cc=200) 15; Bhâg., V. xx. 39; Sha. Ka., *Sub voce*; Chatur Va. Chi. Ma., I. 233. 7, &c.

Dik is not Space, if by that is meant an expanse, extension or room. Space in this sense, and if conceived as a Reality not as a mere and absolute Nothing, is Âkâsha in which all things exist as in a *locality* (Prashasta, pp. 88-89). *See* Ballantyne's translation of Nyâ. Sû. with extracts, Book. IV., p. 26 (top).

The Vaish. Sûtra, II. ii. 10, beginning the section on Dik, simply says that the characteristic of Dik is that it is from or on account of it that "there arises the fact that this thing is here or there from this other thing."

It is clear that in this Sûtra only *relative position* of things is alluded to and not their extent or expanse or their occupation of space, *each by itself.*

That this is so will be seen also from Bhâ. Par. 45. Dik would not be unlike 'gravitation' if the latter could be regarded as an independent Reality and not a mere property of things.

26 (p. 63). The arguments on this section (Âtman) are based on the following authorities:—

Vaish. Sû., III. i. 1-6; III. ii. 4, 5, 19-21; with Upask., Vivṛ. and Chan. Bhâṣh. on them.

Nyâ. Sû.
Nyâ. Bhâṣh.
Nyâ Vâr.
N. V. T. Ṭ.
Nyâ Vṛit. } **I. i. 10.**
III. i. 10, 16-26, 35-42.
ii. 19 (Vṛit. only).

Prashasta, pp. 99 and 100, with Kandalî on it.

Ki. Va. on same (in Mss).

Saptap., with Mit., pp. 18 and 19.

Nyâ. Mañj., pp. 437 *et seq* and 467 *et seqq*.

Sâṅkh. Sû. with Vijñân, and Ani, III. 20-22; V. 129 or 130.

Shâr. Bhâṣh., III. iii. 54.

Bhâmatî, Intro., ph. 2 and 3, and on III. iii. 54.

Vivaraṇop., pp., 108 and 109.

Cha. Kâ, Vol. II., pp. 132-201; Vol. V., pp. 2 *et seq.*

All that is said in this section is to be found in these texts, but of course arranged and expressed differently.

27 (p. 74). In India it is the heart, rather than the brain, which has been thought to be the direct organ of life. *See*, besides numerous Upaninṣhad passages, Nyâ. Mañj., p. 469.

28 (p. 76). The arguments given here are based on Cha. Kâ., Vol. II., pp. 168-172, where it is shown how the body of one stage is *not*, *as a body*, *i.e.*, as an organic whole, the upâdânas or ingredients of the body at the next stage, but that *some* of the upâdânas only of one body are the upâdânas of another.

29 (p. 87). These are the special doctrines of Nyâya-Vaiṣh.

30 (p. 88). The arguments in support of Manas are based on:—

Vaish. Sû., III. ii 1-3; VII. i. 23; with Upask., Vivṛ., and Chan. Bhâsh. on same.

Nyâ. Sû.
Nyâ. Bhâṣh.
Nyâ. Vâr.
N. V. T. Ṭ.
Nyâ. Vṛit.
} **I. i. 16. III. ii. 59-62.**

Prashasta, with Kandalî, pp. 89-93.
Ki. Va. on same (MSS).
Nyâ. Mañj., p. 498, lines 3-16.

31 (p. 95). The beginninglessness of Saṁsâra is taken for granted and admitted repeatedly in works on Nyâya-Vaish., as will be seen from the references given. But it is not reasoned out as in Brah. Sû., Shâr. Bhâṣh, and other texts.

32 (p. 96). On the use of Saṁsâra in this sense see Shâr. Bhâṣh., II. i. 36, towards the end, beginning with 'Smṛitâvapi.'

33 (p. 97). This is based on Shaṅkara's argument showing how achetana-pradhâna cannot possibly move of itself.

34 (p. 98). Based on Shâr. Bhâṣh., II. i. 33, beginning with Na cha svabhâva, etc., with Rat. Pr. on it.

35. (p. 98) This is a general question asked by all Hindus.

36 (p. 100). The Worlds here are spoken of broadly as of two orders, sensible and super-sensible. The Hindus divide them into several sub-orders.

Part of the arguments in this respect is based on Bṛih. Up., I. IV. 10, with Shaṅkara's commentary on it.

37 (p. 102). This is only the Nyâya-Vaish. division, the Sâṅkhya and the Vedânta analyse the Manas further and recognise several sub-divisions in it. They also eliminate certain features from the Âtman as conceived by the Nyâya-Vaish., and relegate them to the region of Mind.

38 (pp. 103 and 104). I have used the word Saṁskâra here in the sense which it generally bears.

Nyâ. Bhâṣh. uses it as almost synonymous with dharmâdharma, *i.e.*, Adṛiṣhṭa (IV. i. 47). But in Vaish., a distinction is made between Saṁskâra and Adṛiṣhṭa. This kind of Saṁskâra, in the Vaisheṣhika sense, is called Bhâvanâ. Nyâ. Vâr. says Anubandha is another name for Saṁskâra (III. i. 19).

Adṛiṣhṭa is merely postponed Karma and is a common name for Dharma and Adharma. *See* Nyâ. Sû., IV. i. 44-47.

39 (p. 108). The potential in this connection should not be understood in the Sâṅkhya sense but in the sense in which the fruit of a tree is said to be potential in Nyâ. Sû. and Nyâ. Bhâṣh., IV. i. 47. *See* also Nyâ. Sû. and Bhâṣh., IV. i. 50.

40 (p. 110). Practically the full doctrine of Re-incarnation with all that it *implies* is given in Prashasta (loc. cit.). I have only arranged the implied ideas differently.

41 (p. 111). The doctrine of postponed Adṛiṣhṭa is specially taught in the Vedânta which calls it Sañchita Karma. But Nyâ. Bhâṣh., Prashasta, etc., also speak of it as Pûrva-Karma.

42 (p. 113). The idea of 'special gift' to a believer in Re-incarnation and Karma and justice in the universe is a great anomaly.

43 (p. 114) This is based on common Hindu ideas like those contained in the Smṛiti passage which Vijñâna Bhikṣhu quotes in his Bhâṣhya on Sâṅkh. Sû. III. 3.

44 (p. 116). The argument that an embodiment cannot come about all of a sudden and without any reason is based on the section on Animittatâ in Nyâ.

Sû., IV. i. 22-24, with Bhâṣh. and Vârt. on the same; and also on Nyâ. Mañj., p. 470, lines 5 *et seq.*

45 (p. 118). The arguments against heredity are advanced only in modern times by living Hindus. There could be no occasion for such arguments in the past as the ancient Hindus never heard of any such idea.

46 (p. 122). On the idea that all experiencing beings are in reality Âtmans, see Prashasta on 'Creation and Destruction.' There he speaks of all beings, high and low (uchchavâcha), as being created according to their various Karma or Âshaya. But Âshaya is a thing which belongs to Âtmans only.

47 (p. 123). The idea of a hierarchy is most common. That is how Indra, for instance, is spoken of as Devarâja.

48 (pp. 56 and 125). Prashasta says that Brahmâ was ordered to create the universal order of things. This would seem to mean that the universe was not due to Brahmâ's Adṛiṣhṭa. But he also speaks of the Universe coming to an end when the time comes for Brahmâ's Freedom (Apavarga). This can only mean that during his life, *i.e.*, the existence of the Universe, Brahmâ is not Free, namely from Adṛiṣhṭa. And if he has Adṛiṣhṭa, then it is obvious that the Universe is produced by it. In any case it is a common Hindu idea that one can rise to be a Brahmâ (*i.e.*, gain Brahmatva) by his Karma. *See* Nîlakaṇṭha on Ma. Bhâr., I. 64. 43.

49 (p. 128). The period of Sṛiṣhṭi alone is also called a Kalpa. The name is significant inasmuch as it implies that the Universe is due to the *imagination* of Brahman. *See* Ki. Va. on Sṛiṣhṭi-Saṁhâra.

50 (p. 129). On 'Nothing new under the sun,' *see* Vivṛ., IX. ii. 7; Shâr. Bhâṣh., I. iii. 30. It is a common Hindu idea.

51 (p. 130). This too is a common idea. It is the Ṛiṣhis and other great beings who appear first and help and guide others. Many of the texts already referred to will support this. For instance, Prashasta on Sṛiṣhṭi-Saṁhâra (towards end.)

52 (p. 130). This follows as an inevitable conclusion from what has gone before.

53 (p. 131). Eternity of the Veda from the Nyâya-Vaish. point of view does not mean that the words (shabda) of the Veda are eternal. But the Veda as *wisdom* is eternal inasmuch as it has always existed and come down from age to age and from teacher to pupil. *See* Nyâ. Bhâṣh., II. i. 68 (last Sûtra), towards end.

It will be noticed that I have not alluded to the idea that the Veda is Îshvara-vâkya, *i.e.*, the word of the Deity. This is not to be found in the original Sûtras. For an explanation, without any reference to Îshvara, of Vaish., I. i. 3, on which that idea is generally based, *see* Chan. Bhâṣh on the same.

54 (p. 132). The idea of Varṇâshrama-Dharma is the very root and foundation of Hindu Society. It constitutes what may be called the Hindu Sociology. What is translated as 'caste' is its embodiment. But it is a question which can scarcely be discussed here at length

55 (p. 132). It is not maintained by the Hindus that there is no happiness or enjoyment in the world, but that all happiness, however great, is ever tinged with suffering

and at best perishable. *See* on this Nyâ. Sû., IV. i. 55-58, with Bhâṣh and Vârt. on the same.

56 (p. 134). Activity is needed to 'purify the heart' (chitta-shuddhi) and this activity consists in doing one's duty (avashya-karaṇîya karma; Kandalî, p. 282, line 10).

57 (p. 140). Philosophy is only Manana Shâstra. *See* Vivṛ., V. ii. 16.

58 (p. 140). Transcendental (Atîndriya) truths cannot be *ascertained* by reasoning, Nyâ. Vâr., II. i. 28 (as counted there, p. 214); Shâr. Bhâṣh., II. i. 11; Shrî-Bhâṣh on the same sûtras, &c. Kapila also taught the Sâṅkhya, not by knowing it as a matter of speculation, but by direct experience. He was a *Siddha* (Bhag. Gîtâ, X. 26; Tattvasamâsa Ṭîkâ, opening part). And candidates following the Sâṅkhaya standard also realise truth by experience. *See* Sâṅkh. Sû. I. 59; XI. 3; VI. 28, 29, &c.

59 (p. 141). All Hindu systems start with the idea of helping man to understand practices or truths so that, by following the former or realising the latter, he may either gain happiness in some specific state of existence or be absolutely free. Thus their object is practical. *See* the beginnings of all standard works on the Darshanas. The Bhâṣhya on Karma-Mîmâṁsâ says: "Sa hi (dharmaḥ) niḥshreyasena puruṣhaṁ saṁyunaktîti pratijânîmahe." I. i. 1. (end). Of course, 'Niḥshreyasa' here means existence in a high state in the universal hierarchy. *See* Cha. Kâ, Vol. I., pp. 105 and 6 on this.

60 (p. 141). For an illustration of how theoretical, *i.e.*, merely inferential knowledge, or mere faith cannot remove suffering, *see* Ki. Va., p. 11, with Ki. Va. Pr. on it. The example is of what is called 'diṅmoha.'

61 (144). That Buddhists also are at one with the Hindus on this point will be seen, for instance, from Dîgh. Nik., Sâm.-Phala-Sutta (2) or Maj. Nik., Mahâ-Assapura-Sutta (39), and numerous other places.

62 (p. 144). The idea that Yoga means a dull state is due perhaps to the misunderstanding of Patañjali's definition of it.

63 (p. 145). Of course all Yoga must be preceded by Karma-Yoga, which means activity. Even attempts at realising Samâdhi by sitting still do not imply idleness but involve intense effort on the part of the aspirant. Comp. the Buddhist practice of Sammâvâyâmo.

64 (p. 146). The *mere* preliminaries which are absolutely indispensable include the highest of moral virtues. *See* Yoga Sû., II. 30 and 31. A Yogin means one who practises, or has mastered, Yoga.

65 (p. 148). On this *see* the Bhag. Gîtâ , Chaps. II-V, where the preliminaries of practising Samâdhi, *i.e.*, perfect concentration, are discussed. The Samâdhi is taught in Chap. VI.

66 (p. 149). On the realisation of the Paramâṇus, Âkâsha, &c., *see* Nyâ. Bhâṣh., IV. ii. 2. There is a remarkable work on the subject by a living Sannyâsin of great learning and saintliness of character. The name of the work is Sâṅkhya-tattvâloka and of the author, Hariharânanda Âraṇya (Sannyâsin name).

67 (p. 151). I say that the supposed Euclidean step may be said to correspond to Yoga *only in a way*, because such a step would give one a direct knowledge, by experience, *not* of a general proposition as such—as, for instance, ' three angles of any triangle are equal

to 180 degrees '—but only in regard to a particular case or a number of cases which may be examined experimentally. Yoga, on the contrary, enables one to acquire a direct experience of the truth of even general propositions. How this is possible can be made clear only by a full consideration of the true nature of general truths or general ideas as distinguished from concrete ideas and facts and by showing how the former also exist as facts independently of the latter. Indeed this would mean a full consideration of the Vaisheṣhika doctrines of the Sâmânya and Visheṣha (*i.e.*, Generality and Particularity) which together with that of the Samavâya, *i.e.*, absolutely inseparable and intimate Relation or absolute concomitance have been left out in this essay. See *ante*, Preface, p. v, last para. *See* also Appendix C.

68 (p. 151). On the sameness of goal of all the systems, *see* Ât. T. Viv., p. 1.

69 (p. 152). In regard to the necessity or otherwise of the realisation of secondary truths, *see* Sâṅkh. T. L., just referred to, and Shi. Dh., pp. 58-61.

THE END.

APPENDIX A.

My very dear and philosophic friend, Mr. B. Keightley, M.A. (Cantab.), Bar-at-law, to whom I am most grateful for going through the proofs of this volume as well as for several suggestions and much valuable criticism, has written as follows:—

"The Adṛishṭa or *Moral* merit and demerit attaching to the Âtmans imply necessarily some standard or definite criterion and scale of morality. Now it is universally accepted in modern philosophic discussion in the West, that *morality* (of any kind or order) *can only arise* in a 'society' of conscious interacting beings, it being held and granted by all that morality is through and through a *social* thing. The only possible alternative (now abandoned mostly) being that morality is determined by the *Will* of a personal God.

"Now as Âtmans are everlasting and Adṛiṣṭa attaches to them *per se* and not as the result of any *fiat* of a personal God: How does the *moral* element come in and what is the moral *standard*, the moral criterion? And how *can* there be any such in respect of Âtmans which (in Hindu Realism) do not apparently possess self-consciousness *as such*, nor are they spoken of as ultimately 'forming a society'?

"At least the point raised ought to be noticed, I think, however briefly."

It is not only this one question but several others also which have been left out of consideration in this essay which is intended to be but a short introduction to only the metaphysics of the system. Still as the point has been raised, it may just briefly be touched upon as suggested by my friend. Of course, anything like a full discussion of the question is quite impossible here, as it touches upon the whole subject of Ethical philosophy from the Hindu point of view. Briefly, then, the Hindu ideas in this respect may be stated as follows :—

(*a*) The Hindu philosopher would be disposed to agree with the Western thinker in saying 'that morality is through and through a *social* thing,' but with an important reservation, *viz.*:—

That while morality is a social thing, moral conduct (including both action and thoughts and feelings) has, from the Hindu point of view, for its real objective *not* 'others' but oneself whom it is intended to benefit primarily, any benefit accruing from such conduct to 'others' being only secondary and incidental, even though *inevitable* because, from the Hindu point of view, no conduct can be for the real and true and absolute benefit of oneself unless it is also beneficial—at any rate harmless—to 'others.'

The idea that one is leading a '*moral*' or *virtuous* life solely for the benfit of 'others' is, from the Hindu point of view, a pure delusion. From their standpoint no conduct is 'moral' or 'virtuous' which has solely 'others' as its objective. If or when such conduct is possible, it ceases to be moral. If anything, it then becomes super-moral. For it is possible *only* when a being has reached a stage in his existence wherein he can be himself affected neither by the doing of a moral act (whether an actual performance or merely in thought and feeling) *nor by its omission* ; that is to say, when he has realised Mokṣha or true and final Freedom and Independence (see *ante*, pp. 133 *et seq.*). Short of that stage, 'moral conduct' is *essential* and *absolutely necessary* for an experiencing being—necessary, because if he does *not* follow it he will *harm* himself by 'degrading' his nature and by bringing about his fall from the 'moral' height where he may have reached, if not by checking his further advancement. It is really with this thought, however secretly and sub-consciously cherished in one's heart, of avoiding the risk of 'degradation' on one's own part, if not of positively retarding one's moral and spiritual status, that all beings below the Mokṣha stage endeavour to lead a moral life.

The real objective of 'moral conduct' therefore, is one's own self.

(*b*) This being the nature of 'moral conduct' from the Hindu point of view, 'morality,' *i.e.*, Dharma, may be defined (as has been hinted above, p. 107 and as is indeed done by the Vaisheṣhika) as the conduct,—including both outward actions and thinking and feeling,—which makes for the advancement of an experiencing entity in the scale of existence in specific forms, or which ultimately leads to (or serves as an intermediate means of realising) absolute Freedom, *i.e.*, Mokṣha (Yato' bhyudaya-niḥshreyasasiddhiḥsa dharmaḥ; Vaish. Sû., I. i. 2.)

(*c*) Under these circumstances, the moral element comes in the fact that an experiencing being may or may not follow such a line of conduct as would make for its progress upward in the scale of beings, or would conduce to the acquisition of that direct experience of the truth of the real nature of things which enables one to realise Freedom. If he does not follow such conduct then there is degradation and suffering for him, —degradation and suffering which are, on the one hand, brought about, in virtue of Samavâya, as the inevitable consequences (either immediately or when opportunity offers, the consequences abiding in the meantime as Adṛiṣhṭa or potential worth) of violating the Dharma, *i.e.*, the rules of moral conduct at any given stage and occasion; and, on the other, teach the experiencer the necessity of not violating the Dharma again, the lessons thus taught being noted down and retained as indelible Saṁskâras (*ante*, pp. 103 to 106), not so much in the surface consciousness as in the innermost depths of the Soul (in the subliminal or subconscious Self, in the language of modern Western thought).

(*d*) And the Moral *Standard* is furnished by the Universal Experience of the past, retained as the Universal Wisdom or the Veda by the being or beings in the higher and highest specific forms of existence, *i.e.*, by Brahmâ and the Ṛishis who, from their own experiences in the past, can, and as a matter of fact do, lay down the rules of Dharma or Moral Conduct, teaching experiencing beings how they should behave if they want to progress higher and higher in the scale of specific forms of existence or to realise Freedom—teaching them how they should avoid harming *others* (though for their own sakes), how they should not tell lies, *i.e.*, misrepresent facts and real intentions and thus mislead *others*; and so on,

(Comp. Tad-vachanât Âmnâyasya prâmâṇyam ; Vaish. Sû., I. i. 3 or 4).

(*e*) Finally, the Âtmans do form a Society, indeed a hierarchy of the Universe, as shown above (p. 123).

It is only when they cease *finally* to have embodiments, *i.e.*, die the last of deaths *after* they have attained Mokṣha by realising, by direct experience, the truths of the essential nature of things, and thus *cease* to have any Adṛiṣhṭas, that they cease also to be 'social' beings in the sense that they then have no *necessity* of forming part of the 'Univeral Society.' But then, when thus Freed, they also cease to be under any moral obligation —they become Super-moral as said before. Till then they *are* conscious of and experience *specific things* and constitute a Society of 'Souls,' whether incarnate in physical bodies or discarnate but still existing as limited beings in specific forms even though these may be super-physical.

APPENDIX B.

Mr. Keightley suggested also that I should avoid using the words 'Polyonymism' and 'Polyonymic' as names of the third Standard, and I would have done so if it were not too late. But the sense in which I have used the terms is quite clear, I think, from what is said on p. 16 *ante.* In case, however, this may not be so, it may be explained here that, what I mean by Polyonymism is the doctrine which holds that what is experienced as the Universe is essentially a single, uniform Reality of the nature of pure Intelligence or Experiencing Principle, without there being in it or as part of it anything of the nature of the *experienced,*—this Single Reality *appearing* under what is but a *multiplicity* of *names, i.e.,* ideas *as such* and ideas *objectified* (called respectively Nâma or 'name' and Rûpa or Form). The doctrine could be called Idealism, if these 'names,' which constitute the Universe when substantiated by the Reality underlying them, formed any part of the Real. This, however, is not regarded to be the case; *i.e.,* not regarded by the typical school representing the third Standard, *viz.,* the Vedânta, even though there are other schools belonging to this Standard which do regard the 'Name' (or 'Names and Forms') as part of the Real.

Besides, the second Standard also is a form of Idealism, inasmuch as the material or the physical (*i.e.,* the sensible) is regarded by it as derived from what are really of the nature of thoughts and feelings; and it would not therefore do to call the third Standard also 'idealism.'

APPENDIX C.

The qualification, hinted at by the phrase "in a way only" on p. 151 and explained in Note 67, owes its origin to Dr. J. E. McTaggart, Fellow of Trinity College, Cambridge, to whom I am deeply indebted for much valuable help. In the present instance, it was he who first pointed out to me how the statement as originally made in the paragraph under reference was defective. It was then only that the qualifying phrase was introduced and the note on it written.